Thailand Travel Guide 2025-2026

Your Ultimate Thailand Adventure

Emery Caldwell

Copyright © 2026 Emery Caldwell

All rights reserved. No part of this book may be reproduced, stored in a retrieval system, or transmitted in any form or by any means—electronic, mechanical, photocopying, recording, or otherwise—without prior written permission from the publisher, except for brief quotations in critical reviews or articles.

Table of Contents

Chapter 1: Introduction to Thailand

    1.1 Overview of Thailand: Culture, Geography, and History

    1.2 Best Time to Visit: Seasonal Travel Guide

    1.3 Visa Requirements and Travel Essentials

    1.4 Safety and Travel Tips

Chapter 2: Planning Your Trip to Thailand

    2.1 Booking Flights and Arrival Tips

    2.2 Currency and Banking: Money Exchange and ATMs

    2.3 Transportation within Thailand: Local Travel Options

    2.4 Travel Insurance: What You Need to Know

Chapter 3: Exploring Thailand's Major Cities

    3.1 Bangkok: The Vibrant Capital

    3.2 Chiang Mai: A Cultural Escape

    3.3 Phuket: Beaches, Resorts, and Nightlife

    3.4 Pattaya: Fun and Adventure for All Ages

Chapter 4: Unique Experiences and Activities

    4.1 Thailand's Beautiful Islands: Exploring Krabi, Koh Samui, and Koh Phi Phi

    1. Krabi: Adventure and Serenity in Nature

    2. Koh Samui: Luxury, Beaches, and Wellness

    3. Koh Phi Phi: Iconic Beauty and Adventure

4.2 Adventure and Sports: Hiking, Diving, and More
1. Hiking and Trekking in Thailand
2. Scuba Diving and Snorkeling
3. Water Sports and Beach Activities
4. Rock Climbing

4.3 Thai Cuisine: A Culinary Journey
1. Key Ingredients in Thai Cooking
2. Must-Try Dishes in Thai Cuisine
3. Regional Specialties
4. Thai Street Food Culture
5. Cooking Classes: Learn to Make Thai Food
6. Thai Beverage and Desserts

4.4 Festivals and Events: Must-See Thai Celebrations
1. Songkran Festival (Thai New Year)
2. Loy Krathong Festival
3. Yi Peng Lantern Festival
4. Chinese New Year
5. Vegetarian Festival (Tesagan Gin Je)
6. Loy Krathong Yi Peng (Lantern Festival) in Sukhothai
7. King's and Queen's Birthday Celebrations

Chapter 5: Accommodation in Thailand
5.1 Hotels: Luxury, Mid-Range, and Budget Options
1. Luxury Hotels and Resorts
2. Mid-Range Hotels

3. Budget Hotels and Guesthouses

4. Hostels and Homestays

5.2 Unique Stays: Eco-Resorts, Floating Hotels, and Villas

1. Eco-Resorts: Sustainable Luxury Amid Nature

2. Floating Hotels and Resorts: Stay on the Water

3. Private Villas: Exclusivity and Luxury

4. Unique and Themed Stays

5.3 Hostels and Guesthouses: A Backpacker's Guide

1. What to Expect from Hostels and Guesthouses in Thailand

2. Popular Hostel and Guesthouse Destinations

    Bangkok

    Chiang Mai

    Koh Phi Phi

    Pai

    Koh Samui

3. Tips for Booking Hostels and Guesthouses in Thailand

5.4 Booking Tips: How to Find the Best Deals

1. Use Multiple Booking Platforms

2. Book Early for Popular Destinations

3. Look for Deals on Last-Minute Booking Apps

4. Consider Alternative Accommodations

5. Take Advantage of Special Promotions and Discounts

6. Read Reviews and Look for Hidden Fees

7. Stay Outside of Popular Tourist Areas
8. Consider Longer Stays for Better Rates

Chapter 6: Cultural Etiquette and Local Customs
- 6.1 Respecting Thai Culture: Do's and Don'ts
- 1. The Do's of Thai Culture
  - 1.1. Dress Modestly When Visiting Temples
  - 1.2. Wai Gesture (Traditional Greeting)
  - 1.3. Show Respect to the Royal Family
  - 1.4. Show Respect to Elders
  - 1.5. Use Polite Language and Behavior
- 2. The Don'ts of Thai Culture
  - 2.1. Don't Touch the Head
  - 2.2. Don't Point Your Feet
  - 2.3. Don't Raise Your Voice or Publicly Lose Your Temper
  - 2.4. Don't Engage in Public Displays of Affection
  - 2.5. Don't Point at People or Objects
- 3. General Cultural Etiquette Tips
- 6.2 Understanding Thai Religion: Buddhism and Temples
- 1. Buddhism in Thailand: An Overview
- 2. Temples (Wats) in Thailand: Sacred Spaces and Cultural Heritage
  - 2.1. Key Elements of a Thai Temple
  - 2.2. Common Buddha Statues and Their Meanings
- 3. Visiting Temples in Thailand: Etiquette and

Respect
- 3.1. Dress Modestly
- 3.2. Remove Your Shoes
- 3.3. Don't Touch the Buddha Images
- 3.4. Show Respect to Monks
- 3.5. Maintain a Calm and Quiet Demeanor
- 3.6. Make Offerings and Donations

4. The Role of Monks in Thai Society

5. Buddhist Holidays and Festivals in Thailand

6.3 Dress Code: What to Wear in Different Settings

1. Dress Code for Visiting Temples and Religious Sites
   - 1.1. General Guidelines for Temples:
   - 1.2. Specific Examples of What to Wear

2. Dress Code for Beach and Island Visits
   - 2.1. Beachwear Guidelines:
   - 2.2. Example of Beachwear Etiquette

3. Dress Code for Urban Areas (Bangkok, Chiang Mai, etc.)
   - 3.1. General City Etiquette:
   - 3.2. Example of Urban Attire

4. Dress Code for Rural Areas and Villages
   - 4.1. Modesty and Respect for Local Traditions
   - 4.2. Example of Rural Attire

5. Dress Code for Special Events and Festivals

6.4 Language: Basic Thai Phrases for Travelers

1. Basic Greetings and Courtesies

- 1.1. Hello and Goodbye
- 1.2. Thank You
- 1.3. How Are You?
- 1.4. Goodbye
2. Polite Expressions
    - 2.1. Excuse Me / Sorry
    - 2.2. Yes
    - 2.3. No
    - 2.4. Please
3. Ordering Food and Drinks
    - 3.1. I Would Like
    - 3.2. How Much is This?
    - 3.3. Delicious
    - 3.4. Water
    - 3.5. Food
4. Directions and Transportation
    - 4.1. Where is…?
    - 4.2. How Do I Get to…?
    - 4.3. Taxi
    - 4.4. Bus
5. Numbers and Currency
    - 5.1. Numbers 1-10
    - 5.2. Prices
6. Emergency Phrases
    - 6.1. Help!
    - 6.2. I'm Lost
    - 6.3. I Need a Doctor
    - 6.4. Where is the Police?

Chapter 7: Shopping, Nightlife, and Entertainment

7.1 Markets and Shopping: From Street Stalls to Malls

1. Street Markets: The Heart of Thai Shopping Culture
1.1. Chatuchak Weekend Market (Bangkok)
1.2. Night Markets
1.3. Floating Markets

2. Modern Shopping Malls: Luxury and Global Brands
2.1. Siam Paragon (Bangkok)
2.2. CentralWorld (Bangkok)
2.3. ICONSIAM (Bangkok)

3. Bargaining: Haggling in Thailand's Markets
3.1. How to Bargain

7.2 Nightlife: Bars, Clubs, and Shows in Thailand

1. Bars and Pubs: Relaxed and Lively Spots for Socializing
1.1. Rooftop Bars: Breathtaking Views and Chic Atmospheres
1.2. Beach Bars and Island Bars: Relaxed Vibes by the Sea
1.3. Craft Beer and Pub Bars

2. Nightclubs: Dance the Night Away
2.1. EDM and Dance Clubs
2.2. Live Music Venues

3. Shows and Cultural Performances
3.1. Traditional Thai Shows

3.2. Cabaret Shows

7.3 Thai Massage and Spas: Relaxation at Its Best

1. Traditional Thai Massage

    1.1. What to Expect from Thai Massage

    1.2. The Process of Thai Massage

    1.3. Best Places for Traditional Thai Massage

2. Spa Treatments in Thailand: Luxury and Wellness

    2.1. Popular Spa Treatments

    2.2. Luxury Spas in Thailand

    2.3. Thai Spa Experience at Hotels and Resorts

3. Unique Wellness Experiences in Thailand

    3.1. Meditation and Mindfulness

    3.2. Detox and Wellness Retreats

7.4 Entertainment for Families: Theme Parks and Cultural Shows

1. Theme Parks: Fun for All Ages

    1.1. Dream World (Bangkok)

    1.2. Siam Park City (Bangkok)

    1.3. Cartoon Network Amazone Waterpark (Pattaya)

    1.4. Safari World (Bangkok)

    1.5. Khao Kheow Open Zoo (Chonburi)

2. Cultural Shows and Performances: A Window into Thai Traditions

    2.1. Siam Niramit (Bangkok)

    2.2. Cultural Shows in Chiang Mai: Khantoke Dinner and Traditional Dance

2.3. Phuket FantaSea (Phuket)
2.4. Thai Puppet Shows: Traditional Thai Puppetry (Bangkok and Chiang Mai)

Chapter 1: Introduction to Thailand

1.1 Overview of Thailand: Culture, Geography, and History

Culture

Thailand is a country rich in culture, combining ancient traditions with a modern flair. Thai culture is influenced by several factors, including religion, monarchy, and local customs. The majority of the population practices Theravada Buddhism, which plays an important role in shaping daily life. Temples, or "wats," are abundant throughout the country, serving as both spiritual centers and community hubs. Thai people are known for their warmth and hospitality, and visitors are often welcomed with a friendly "wai," a traditional greeting where hands are pressed together in prayer-like fashion.

The monarchy holds a revered place in Thai society, with King Maha Vajiralongkorn being the current monarch. The royal family is deeply respected, and it is common to see portraits of the king displayed throughout the country. The Thai government encourages respect for the monarchy, and any form of disrespect toward the monarchy is considered highly inappropriate and is illegal under lèse-majesté laws.

Traditional Thai art and architecture are deeply influenced by Buddhism, as seen in the intricate designs of temples and shrines. Thai dance, music, and literature also draw from Buddhist teachings and royal patronage. Contemporary Thai culture is an eclectic mix of traditional influences with modern elements, especially in the urban centers where fashion, technology, and international influence have a significant presence.

Geography

Thailand, located in Southeast Asia, is bordered by Myanmar to the northwest, Laos to the northeast, Cambodia to the southeast, and Malaysia to the south. It also has coastlines along the Gulf of Thailand and the Andaman Sea. The country is divided into four main regions: the Central Plains, the North, the Northeast (Isaan), and the South.

The Central Plains, where Bangkok is located, are fertile and home to much of the country's agriculture. This area is often referred to as the "Rice Bowl" of Thailand due to its abundant rice production. To the north lies the mountainous region of Chiang Mai, Chiang Rai, and other northern provinces, which are known for their cooler climate, lush forests, and historic hill tribe communities. The Northeast, also known as Isaan, is a relatively arid region with rich cultural heritage, offering a contrast to the tropical lushness of the south.

Thailand's southern region is known for its world-renowned beaches, islands, and resort areas. Famous islands such as Koh Samui, Koh Phi Phi, and

Koh Tao attract tourists from all over the world. The country also boasts a diverse array of wildlife, from elephants in the north to tigers and various marine life species in the south.

History

Thailand has a long and rich history that dates back thousands of years. It was originally home to several ancient civilizations, such as the Dvaravati and Srivijaya Kingdoms. However, the modern history of Thailand can be traced back to the establishment of the Kingdom of Siam in the 13th century. The first Thai kingdom, the Sukhothai Kingdom, was founded in 1238 and is considered the birthplace of Thai culture, including the development of the Thai alphabet and the establishment of Buddhism as the state religion.

Following the Sukhothai period, the Ayutthaya Kingdom emerged as a dominant power from the 14th to the 18th century. Ayutthaya, located in central Thailand, grew into a prosperous city-state with strong trade relations, particularly with China, Japan, and European countries. The kingdom was eventually destroyed by the Burmese in 1767, leading to the establishment of the Kingdom of Thonburi, which was later replaced by the current Chakri dynasty under King Rama I in 1782. This marked the beginning of the modern era for Thailand.

In the 19th and early 20th centuries, Thailand successfully navigated the pressures of Western colonization, remaining one of the few Southeast Asian countries to avoid imperial domination. Under King Chulalongkorn (Rama V), Thailand modernized its economy, military, and infrastructure, becoming a constitutional monarchy in the early 20th century.

The 20th century was marked by significant political upheaval, including the 1932 revolution that transformed the country from an absolute monarchy to a constitutional monarchy. The country also experienced periods of military rule and coups, yet has maintained its identity as a sovereign nation with a deep connection to its cultural and royal roots.

Thailand officially changed its name from Siam to Thailand in 1939, reflecting a new national identity that embraced all ethnic groups in the country, though the majority remains ethnically Thai. The modern political landscape of Thailand has been shaped by a mix of democracy, military coups, and a complex relationship with its monarchy.

In recent decades, Thailand has emerged as a major player in Southeast Asia, with a strong economy driven by agriculture, manufacturing, and tourism. The country's political scene remains dynamic and often turbulent, but Thailand continues to be one of the most visited destinations in the world, attracting millions of tourists each year with its unique blend of natural beauty, rich history, and cultural heritage.

1.2 Best Time to Visit: Seasonal Travel Guide

Thailand is a tropical country, and its weather varies depending on the region and time of year. To get the most out of your trip, understanding the seasonal patterns is crucial. Thailand has three main seasons: the cool season, the hot season, and the rainy season. Each season offers a different experience, making it important to choose the right time to visit based on your interests.

Cool Season (November to February)

The cool season is generally considered the best time to visit Thailand, particularly for those who are new to the country or looking to explore all it has to offer without the extreme heat or heavy rainfall. During these months, the weather is most pleasant, with lower humidity and cooler temperatures, especially in the northern and central regions. In Bangkok, Chiang Mai, and other cities in the north, temperatures typically range from 25°C to 30°C (77°F to 86°F), which is comfortable for sightseeing and outdoor activities.

This period also coincides with many of Thailand's major festivals, such as **Loy Krathong** (usually in November), where people release floating lanterns on rivers in a beautiful display of lights, and **Songkran** (the Thai New Year in mid-April), marked by water fights and street celebrations. However, note that Songkran falls just outside the cool season, in the hot season.

The cool season is also a great time to visit the islands and beaches, as the weather is warm and dry, ideal for activities such as snorkeling, diving, and lounging on the beach. Popular destinations like **Koh Samui**, **Phuket**, and **Krabi** see a peak in tourism during this period, making it lively but also more crowded. Booking accommodations and tours in advance is recommended.

Hot Season (March to June)
The hot season, especially from March to May, can be intense, with daytime temperatures regularly exceeding 35°C (95°F) in many parts of the country. This is the time when the weather is hottest, especially in the central plains and northern regions. While it may be too hot for some travelers to fully enjoy outdoor activities, this period is ideal for those looking to visit the islands, especially those in the Gulf of Thailand such as **Koh Samui**, **Koh Phangan**, and **Koh Tao**, where the temperatures are relatively milder.

If you choose to visit during this time, be sure to stay hydrated, wear sunscreen, and schedule outdoor activities for early mornings or late afternoons to avoid the midday heat. Despite the high temperatures, this is also a great time to take advantage of hotel promotions and discounted prices, as this is considered the low season in some areas.

One notable event during this season is **Songkran**, celebrated in April, which is the Thai New Year and involves massive water fights and traditional ceremonies. If you're in Thailand during this time, it's an experience you won't want to miss. It's important to remember that Songkran can cause disruptions in some areas due to street celebrations, so it might not be ideal for travelers looking for a peaceful, quiet vacation.

Rainy Season (July to October)
The rainy season, or the monsoon season, lasts from June to October, with the heaviest rains usually occurring from August to September. During this period, Thailand experiences frequent showers, though rain typically falls in the form of short but heavy downpours, often in the afternoon or evening. Despite the rain, this season is not a complete washout, and many travelers still visit during this time.

The rainy season offers a more serene experience with fewer tourists, lower prices, and lush, green landscapes. It is a great time to explore Thailand's natural beauty, as the jungles, waterfalls, and forests are at their most vibrant. The northern and central regions, including places like **Chiang Mai** and **Chiang Rai**, benefit from cooler temperatures due to the rain, making it a more pleasant time for trekking and visiting the mountains.

The southern islands on the Andaman Sea, such as **Phuket** and **Krabi**, tend to experience more rainfall than those on the Gulf side, such as **Koh Samui** and **Koh Phangan**, which are slightly drier. However, even in the rainy season, the beaches and islands are still enjoyable, and the rain doesn't usually last long enough to ruin your plans. The quieter beaches and resorts also mean more relaxation and fewer crowds.

If you don't mind the rain and are looking for a more budget-friendly and peaceful vacation, this season can be a good choice. It's also the time when many resorts and hotels offer off-peak discounts.

Regional Differences

When planning your visit, it's important to consider that different regions of Thailand experience the weather patterns in different ways. The central plains, where Bangkok and Ayutthaya are located, experience the most extreme heat in the hot season and the heaviest rainfall during the monsoon. The north, including cities like Chiang Mai and Chiang Rai, enjoys cooler temperatures during the cool season and a comfortable climate in the rainy season. The southern regions, including popular islands like **Phuket** and **Koh Samui**, are slightly more consistent, with rain falling more frequently in the west than in the east.

To sum up, the **cool season (November to February)** is the best time to visit for the most comfortable weather and vibrant festivals. If you don't mind heat and want fewer crowds, the **hot season (March to June)** offers great deals, especially on the islands. Lastly, the **rainy season (July to October)** can be ideal for nature lovers and budget travelers looking for quieter experiences and lower prices.

1.3 Visa Requirements and Travel Essentials

Visa Requirements

Thailand offers a range of visa options depending on your nationality, the purpose of your visit, and the duration of your stay. Understanding the visa requirements beforehand is crucial to ensuring a smooth entry into the country.

- **Visa Exemption**: Citizens of many countries, including the United States, the United Kingdom, Canada, Australia, and most European Union countries, can enter Thailand without a visa for short stays. For tourism purposes, travelers from these countries can stay in Thailand for up to **30 days** if entering by air or **15 days** if entering overland. This visa exemption is typically valid for tourism, business meetings, or transit purposes.

- **Visa on Arrival**: Citizens from certain countries, such as China, India, and several Middle Eastern nations, are eligible for a **Visa on Arrival (VoA)**. This allows a stay of up to **15 days**. The process involves filling out an application at the airport upon arrival and presenting the required documents, including proof of onward travel and sufficient funds for the duration of your stay.

- **Tourist Visa**: If you plan to stay longer than the visa exemption allows, you may need to apply for a **Tourist Visa**. This visa is available for stays of **60 days** and can be extended for an additional **30 days** while in Thailand. It can be obtained through the Thai embassy or consulate in your home country or a neighboring country.

- **Non-Immigrant Visas**: If your visit is for purposes other than tourism, such as business, education, or medical treatment, you may need to apply for a **Non-Immigrant Visa**. This visa is typically valid for **90 days** and can also be extended.

- **Multiple-Entry Tourist Visa (METV)**: For long-term travelers or those who plan to leave and re-enter Thailand multiple times within a year, the **Multiple-Entry Tourist Visa** is an option. This visa allows multiple entries within a **6-month period**, and each stay can last **60 days**, with the possibility of extensions.

It's important to check the latest visa regulations before traveling, as they are subject to change, especially in the post-pandemic era or during special circumstances.

Travel Essentials

Aside from a valid visa, there are other essential items and considerations to keep in mind when planning your trip to Thailand.

- **Passport**: Your passport must be valid for at least **6 months** from the date of entry into Thailand. It's also recommended to carry photocopies of your passport and visa page in case of loss or theft.

- **Travel Insurance**: While not mandatory, travel insurance is highly recommended for visitors to Thailand. Coverage should include medical emergencies, trip cancellations, lost luggage, and theft. Thailand's healthcare system is of high quality, but having insurance can help mitigate unexpected medical costs. Some policies also offer coverage for adventure activities like diving or trekking, which may be important if you plan on engaging in these.

- **Vaccinations and Health Precautions**: Before traveling to Thailand, it's a good idea to consult with your doctor about recommended vaccinations. Common vaccines for travelers to Thailand include Hepatitis A and B, Typhoid, and Tetanus. Additionally, if you're planning to visit rural areas, particularly in the north or near the border regions, a vaccination for Japanese Encephalitis may be advised. Malaria risk is generally low in major tourist areas but may be a concern in more remote locations. Travelers should also be cautious about mosquito bites and may want to carry insect repellent and take malaria prophylaxis if traveling to areas with higher risks.

- **Currency and Money**: Thailand's official currency is the **Thai Baht (THB)**. While credit cards are widely accepted in larger cities and tourist areas, cash is essential for shopping in markets, smaller towns, and rural areas. ATMs are readily available throughout Thailand, but it's advisable to inform your bank before traveling to avoid any issues with accessing funds. Currency exchange services are available at airports, banks, and exchange booths, though rates may vary.

- **Language**: Thai is the official language in Thailand, and while English is widely spoken in tourist areas, especially in larger cities, learning a few basic Thai phrases can be helpful and appreciated by locals. Common phrases like "Sawasdee" (hello), "Khob khun" (thank you), and "Mai pen rai" (it's okay, no problem) can make your interactions more pleasant.

- **Electrical Adapters**: Thailand uses **Type A, B, and C plugs**, and the standard voltage is **220V** with a frequency of **50Hz**. If your devices use a different plug type or voltage, it's advisable to bring an adapter and possibly a voltage converter to ensure your electronics work properly during your stay.

- **SIM Cards and Internet**: Having access to local mobile data and a reliable internet connection is crucial for navigating and communicating while in Thailand. Prepaid SIM cards are available at the airport or from local shops and can be purchased with a range of data plans. International roaming is another option but may be more expensive. Thailand has excellent mobile coverage in most areas, including tourist spots and major cities.

- **Weather-Appropriate Clothing**: The climate in Thailand is hot and humid for most of the year, so lightweight, breathable clothing is recommended. In temples and religious sites, a conservative dress code is required, with covered shoulders and knees. It's advisable to pack comfortable shoes for walking, sunscreen to protect from the sun, and a rain jacket or umbrella if visiting during the rainy season.

- **Local Etiquette and Customs**: Understanding Thai etiquette will help you navigate the country with respect and ease. Some key customs include the **wai** greeting (pressing the palms together in prayer-like fashion), respecting elders, and removing shoes when entering homes or certain establishments. Be mindful of your behavior when visiting religious sites – dress modestly and avoid touching Buddha statues or images of the royal family.

By preparing with these travel essentials, you can ensure a smooth, enjoyable experience in Thailand, allowing you to focus on enjoying all the beauty and culture the country has to offer.

1.4 Safety and Travel Tips

When traveling to Thailand, it's essential to be mindful of both the local laws and general safety considerations to ensure a smooth and enjoyable experience. While Thailand is generally a safe destination for tourists, like any foreign country, it's important to take precautions, especially when navigating unfamiliar environments. Below are some practical tips to help you stay safe during your trip.

General Safety Tips

- **Stay Aware of Your Surroundings**: As with any popular tourist destination, petty crime such as pickpocketing or bag snatching can occur, especially in crowded places like markets, tourist attractions, and on public transportation. Keep your belongings secure and be cautious when withdrawing cash from ATMs. Avoid carrying large sums of money or flashy jewelry, which can attract unwanted attention.

- **Choose Reputable Transportation**: Whether you are taking taxis, tuk-tuks, or rideshare services like Grab, always choose reliable transportation options. It's recommended to use metered taxis or app-based services to avoid overcharging, especially in busy cities like Bangkok. When taking tuk-tuks, agree on the fare in advance, as these can sometimes be prone to inflated pricing. For safer and more convenient transport in cities, Grab is often a better option.

- **Avoid Scams**: Thailand, like many tourist destinations, has its share of scams. Common ones include overcharging for goods or services, "free tour" offers that lead to overpriced shopping, or "fake" government offices that charge tourists for services. Always double-check prices before committing to a purchase or tour, and be cautious of unsolicited offers from strangers, especially around major tourist landmarks.

- **Stay in Well-Lit and Crowded Areas at Night**: While Thailand is relatively safe for tourists, it's wise to avoid walking alone in poorly lit or less populated areas, particularly after dark. Stick to well-lit, busy streets and, if possible, travel with a group or use rideshare services. While incidents are rare, petty crimes like muggings can occur in less busy areas.

Health and Medical Safety

- **Water and Food Safety**: Tap water in Thailand is not always safe to drink, and it's best to stick to bottled water for drinking. Street food is an integral part of Thai culture and an essential experience, but be selective about where you eat. Choose vendors that look clean and have a high turnover of customers, as this indicates fresh and safe food. If you're unfamiliar with street food, opt for cooked foods rather than raw dishes like salads or fresh fruit that could be contaminated.

- **Travel Health Insurance**: Travel insurance is essential when visiting Thailand. While the healthcare system in major cities like Bangkok and Chiang Mai is of high quality, medical services in rural areas may be more limited. Comprehensive travel insurance will cover medical emergencies, including evacuation if needed, and any trip-related disruptions like flight cancellations or lost luggage.

- **Mosquito Protection**: Thailand is home to mosquitoes that can carry diseases like **Dengue fever** and **Malaria**. Although the risk is relatively low in urban areas, it's still important to take precautions, especially if you plan to visit rural or forested regions. Wear long-sleeved clothing and apply insect repellent containing DEET. Consider taking mosquito nets if staying in rural or eco-friendly accommodations.

- **First Aid Kit**: Pack a small first aid kit with basic items like bandages, antiseptic wipes, pain relievers, antihistamines, and any prescription medication you may need. It's always helpful to be prepared for minor cuts, stomach upset, or insect bites. Pharmacies are widely available, and most carry a good range of over-the-counter medications.

Natural Disasters and Weather Awareness

- **Flooding**: Thailand experiences seasonal flooding during the rainy season (May to October), especially in low-lying areas like Bangkok and parts of the south. If you're visiting during this time, stay informed about the weather, avoid areas prone to flooding, and have an emergency evacuation plan in case of heavy rain. Flooding can sometimes disrupt transportation, so always check local weather reports before planning travel around the country.

- **Earthquakes**: Thailand is not generally known for seismic activity, but earthquakes do occasionally occur, particularly in the northern regions near the border with Myanmar and Laos. While the risk of a major earthquake is low, it's still important to familiarize yourself with basic earthquake safety protocols, such as taking cover under sturdy furniture if you feel tremors.

- **Heat Stroke**: The hot season (March to June) in Thailand can see extreme temperatures. It's important to stay hydrated, wear light, breathable clothing, and use sunscreen regularly. Avoid excessive physical activity during the hottest parts of the day (typically from 11 am to 4 pm), and if you feel lightheaded, seek shade or air conditioning immediately.

Cultural Sensitivity and Behavior

- **Respect the Monarchy**: Thailand holds its monarchy in the highest regard. Any form of disrespect toward the royal family, even through speech or actions, is a criminal offense under the country's **lèse-majesté laws**. Always be respectful and avoid discussing the royal family in a negative light, whether in public or private. It's best to keep conversations about politics or the monarchy to a minimum.

- **Dress Modestly When Visiting Temples**: When visiting temples, especially important ones like the **Grand Palace** in Bangkok or **Wat Pho**, dress conservatively. Both men and women should wear clothing that covers their shoulders, arms, and knees. Avoid wearing shorts or sleeveless tops, and be prepared to remove your shoes before entering temple buildings. The dress code is strictly enforced, and failure to adhere to it may result in being denied entry.

- **Take Care with Public Displays of Affection**: Public displays of affection, such as kissing or hugging, are not common in Thai culture and may be viewed as inappropriate, especially in more rural areas. While hand-holding is generally acceptable, try to avoid more intimate actions in public spaces, particularly in religious sites.

- **Buddhism and Religion**: Buddhism is central to Thai culture, and respecting religious customs is essential. When entering temples or monasteries, always remove your shoes, be mindful of the people praying, and maintain a respectful attitude. It's important not to touch Buddhist monks or their robes, as this is considered highly disrespectful, especially if you are a woman.

Emergency Numbers and Contacts

- **Emergency Services**: The emergency number for police in Thailand is **191**. For medical emergencies, dial **1669** for ambulances. The **Fire Department** can be reached at **199**. It's a good idea to keep these numbers handy, as well as the contact information for your embassy or consulate, in case of emergencies.

- **Embassy Contacts**: While Thailand is generally a safe country to visit, it's advisable to have the contact details for your country's embassy or consulate in case you need assistance with legal issues, lost passports, or emergencies. The embassy will also be able to help if you're in need of consular services like notarization or emergency travel documents.

By following these safety and travel tips, you'll be better prepared to navigate Thailand with confidence and enjoy the many incredible experiences the country has to offer. Remember to stay aware, respectful, and cautious, and your trip to Thailand will be a rewarding and unforgettable adventure.

Chapter 2: Planning Your Trip to Thailand

2.1 Booking Flights and Arrival Tips

Booking your flight to Thailand is one of the first steps in planning a successful trip. Whether you are traveling for leisure, business, or to explore, getting the best deals and understanding the arrival process can significantly enhance your overall travel experience. Below are detailed guidelines on booking your flight, finding the best options, and essential arrival tips to help you start your Thai adventure smoothly.

1. Choosing the Right Airport for Your Arrival

Thailand has several international airports, but the two main entry points for most international travelers are **Suvarnabhumi Airport (BKK)** in Bangkok and **Phuket International Airport (HKT)** in Phuket. The choice of airport largely depends on your travel itinerary and the region of Thailand you plan to explore.

- **Suvarnabhumi Airport (BKK):** The main international gateway to Thailand, Suvarnabhumi is located about 25 kilometers east of Bangkok's city center. It is the busiest and largest airport in Thailand, with direct flights arriving from all over the world. If you plan to start your Thailand trip in Bangkok or head to other northern and central destinations, this airport will be your most convenient point of arrival. The airport is well-connected with public transportation, including taxis, Airport Rail Link (a direct train to the city), and buses, making it easy to get into the city center or other parts of the country.

- **Phuket International Airport (HKT)**: Located on the island of Phuket, this airport is the primary entry point for travelers heading to southern Thailand, including beach resorts like Patong, Kata, and Karon, or other islands like Koh Phi Phi and Koh Samui. Although smaller than Suvarnabhumi, Phuket International is an efficient airport that handles a significant number of international flights, especially from Europe and East Asia. Taxis and shuttle services are available to transport passengers to nearby resorts and towns.

- **Other Airports**: Depending on your travel plans, you might also consider flying into other airports such as **Chiang Mai International Airport (CNX)** for the northern regions, **Don Mueang International Airport (DMK)** in Bangkok (which serves many low-cost carriers), or **Krabi International Airport (KBV)** for the Krabi province and its surrounding islands.

2. Finding the Best Flight Deals

When booking flights to Thailand, finding the best deals requires some research and flexibility. Here are a few tips to help you get the most cost-effective options:

- **Book in Advance**: As with most international flights, booking your flight several weeks or even months in advance typically gives you the best chance to find cheaper fares. Aim to book your tickets **3-6 months** ahead of your planned travel date, especially if you are traveling during peak seasons (cool season or holidays like Songkran).

- **Use Flight Search Engines**: Flight search engines such as **Skyscanner**, **Google Flights**, **Kayak**, and **Momondo** allow you to compare flight prices across multiple airlines. You can use these platforms to identify the best deals and view flexible dates to save money. These websites also offer price tracking tools that can alert you when fares drop for your selected routes.

- **Look for Budget Airlines**: Thailand has several budget carriers that operate domestic and international flights. If you are flexible with your travel dates and don't mind lower service levels, budget airlines like **AirAsia**, **Thai Lion Air**, **Nok Air**, and **Thai VietJet Air** can offer incredibly cheap flights. These airlines operate within Thailand and also offer international routes from nearby countries like Malaysia, Singapore, and

Cambodia.

- **Consider Connecting Flights**: While direct flights are convenient, you may save money by booking connecting flights. For example, you could fly to a major hub like Singapore or Kuala Lumpur and then take a connecting flight to Thailand. Some airlines also offer discounted fares for multi-leg flights, which can be a good option if you want to visit more than one destination in Southeast Asia before heading to Thailand.

- **Check for Special Offers and Deals**: Airlines occasionally run promotions and sales, especially during off-peak months or in conjunction with holidays. Keep an eye out for flash sales, airline loyalty rewards, or special discounts offered by travel agencies. Signing up for airline newsletters or following them on social media can help you stay updated on upcoming deals.

3. Understanding Flight Duration and Time Zones

The duration of your flight to Thailand depends on your departure city and the flight route. From major cities in North America or Europe, direct flights can take anywhere from 12 to 16 hours. Flights from Australia or East Asia are typically shorter, ranging from 7 to 9 hours. If you are flying from neighboring Southeast Asian countries, your flight could be as short as 1-4 hours.

Thailand operates on **Indochina Time (ICT)**, which is **UTC +7**. It's important to adjust your watch or devices to the local time upon arrival to avoid confusion. Keep in mind that there is no daylight saving time in Thailand, so the time remains the same throughout the year.

4. Airport Arrival Tips

Upon arriving in Thailand, it's helpful to understand the processes at the airport and how to navigate the first few steps. Here are some important things to keep in mind:

- **Immigration and Visa Control**: After disembarking from your flight, the first step is to go through **immigration**. Have your passport, completed arrival card (which will be provided on your flight or at the airport), and any necessary visa documents ready. If you are from a visa-exempt country, you may only need to show proof of onward travel (return ticket) and sufficient funds for your stay. If you need a visa, head to the appropriate counter to present your visa documents for processing.

- **Baggage Claim**: Once you've passed through immigration, proceed to the baggage claim area.

Check the signs for your flight number and baggage carousel. Be sure to double-check your luggage tag and ensure you collect the correct bags. If your luggage is missing or damaged, report it to the airline's baggage services desk immediately.

- **Customs**: Thailand has specific customs regulations, particularly regarding duty-free items and prohibited goods such as illegal drugs, weapons, and certain plants or animals. If you are carrying any items that need to be declared, be sure to go to the designated **red channel** for customs. Otherwise, proceed through the **green channel** if you have nothing to declare.

- **Currency Exchange**: After passing through customs, you'll likely find currency exchange counters or ATMs available in the arrivals hall. You can exchange a small amount of currency or withdraw cash, but keep in mind that exchange rates at airports are often less favorable than those found at local banks or exchange booths in the city. It's advisable to withdraw a modest amount of cash to cover initial expenses such as transportation.

- **Transportation from the Airport**: Once you have your luggage, you'll need to get from the airport to your accommodation. Here are some common options for airport transfers:

- **Taxis**: Taxis are available at designated taxi stands at all major airports in Thailand. Most airports have a fixed fare system for taxis heading to different districts. Be sure to use the **official taxi queue** to avoid touts, and insist that the driver uses the meter.
- **Airport Rail Link (BKK)**: The **Airport Rail Link** at Suvarnabhumi Airport provides a convenient and affordable way to reach the city center. The train connects the airport to various parts of Bangkok, including **Phaya Thai**, where you can transfer to the Skytrain (BTS) system.
- **Shuttle Services**: Many hotels and resorts offer shuttle services for a fee. If you've pre-arranged accommodation, check with your hotel to see if they offer a pick-up service.
- **Ride-Hailing Apps (Grab)**: Ride-hailing services like **Grab** are widely available in Thailand, especially in Bangkok. You can book a ride from the airport to your destination directly from your smartphone using the Grab app.

- **SIM Cards and Mobile Data**: Upon arrival, consider purchasing a **SIM card** for your phone to have access to mobile data and stay connected during your trip. SIM cards are available at kiosks within the airport, where you can choose from various plans that include data, calls, and text services.

- **Stay Alert and Safe**: Always remain vigilant at the airport and follow any safety guidelines provided by airport staff. Be cautious about your belongings, avoid engaging with aggressive vendors, and be aware of your surroundings.

By booking your flights carefully, understanding the different airports in Thailand, and following these arrival tips, you can ensure that the start of your trip is seamless and stress-free. With some preparation and awareness, you'll be ready to dive into the many exciting experiences Thailand has to offer.

2.2 Currency and Banking: Money Exchange and ATMs

When traveling to Thailand, understanding the local currency and how to manage your finances is crucial for a smooth and hassle-free experience. This section will guide you through Thailand's currency system, money exchange options, and how to access cash while you're in the country.

1. Thai Currency: The Baht (THB)

The official currency of Thailand is the **Baht (THB)**, which is divided into 100 **satang**. Banknotes come in denominations of **20 baht, 50 baht, 100 baht, 500 baht,** and **1,000 baht,** while coins are available in **1 baht, 2 baht, 5 baht,** and **10 baht,** as well as smaller denominations of **25 satang** and **50 satang.**

When exchanging money or making purchases, you'll commonly encounter prices listed in baht. Many establishments, especially in tourist-heavy areas, will accept both cash and card payments, but it's still important to have sufficient baht on hand, especially in more remote regions or for street vendors.

2. Currency Exchange in Thailand

You'll need Thai Baht for most of your purchases, so understanding how to exchange your home currency into baht efficiently is essential. There are several options for currency exchange, each with its pros and cons:

- **Banks**: Banks in Thailand offer currency exchange services, and they generally provide competitive rates. The major banks such as **Siam Commercial Bank (SCB), Kasikornbank (KBank),** and **Bangkok Bank** have branches throughout the country. The rates offered at bank branches tend to be better than those at exchange booths in tourist areas, although some banks may charge a small service fee for the exchange. It's always a good idea to bring your passport when exchanging large amounts of money, as it may be required for identification.

- **Currency Exchange Booths**: Currency exchange booths, commonly located in tourist areas, shopping malls, airports, and major hotels, are a popular choice for travelers. Exchange rates at these booths can vary, but they tend to offer slightly higher rates than banks. However, it's important to check for hidden fees or commissions before finalizing your exchange. A well-known exchange service is **Superrich**, which offers competitive rates and is highly trusted by both locals and tourists.

- **Airports**: While exchanging currency at the airport can be convenient when you first arrive, be aware that airport exchange counters usually offer less favorable exchange rates than banks or booths in the city. If you need to exchange currency at the airport, only exchange a small amount to cover your immediate expenses, such as transportation to your accommodation.

- **Hotels**: Some hotels also offer currency exchange services, but their rates are typically less competitive. It's better to use hotels only for small amounts of exchange, as the rates will likely be higher than those offered at local exchange services or banks.

- **Online Currency Exchange Platforms**: Some online platforms and apps allow you to order currency exchange before you travel. These services often offer competitive rates and can have the currency delivered to your home or a nearby pickup point. It's a convenient option if you want to avoid long queues when you arrive in Thailand, but you may need to plan ahead.

3. Using ATMs in Thailand

ATMs are widely available throughout Thailand, making it easy for travelers to access cash when needed. However, there are some important points to consider when using ATMs to withdraw Thai Baht:

- **ATM Fees**: While using ATMs is convenient, be aware that foreign ATM cards are subject to fees. The Thai banks charge a flat **200 baht fee** (approximately $6 USD) per transaction for international cards, in addition to any fees your home bank may charge for international withdrawals. It's a good idea to withdraw larger sums of cash at once to minimize the impact of these fees.

- **Bank ATM Networks**: The ATMs in Thailand are generally well-maintained and offer multiple language options, including English. Most ATMs are part of the **Thai Bank Consortium** or the **Bank of Ayudhya (Krungsri)** network, which are compatible with international cards like Visa, MasterCard, and Cirrus. Look for ATM machines with the **Visa** or **MasterCard** logo to ensure your card will be accepted. Be cautious when using ATMs at night or in unfamiliar areas to avoid potential safety risks.

- **ATM Withdrawal Limits**: Many ATMs in Thailand have daily withdrawal limits for foreign cards, typically around **20,000 to 30,000 baht** per transaction (approximately $600 - $900 USD). You can usually make multiple withdrawals in one day, but each transaction will incur a separate fee. Be sure to check the limits and fees before proceeding with a withdrawal.

- **Using Debit/Credit Cards**: In major cities and tourist hotspots, credit and debit cards are widely accepted. Most hotels, restaurants, and shops will accept international cards, especially those with the Visa or MasterCard logos. However, smaller businesses and street vendors may prefer cash payments. It's important to notify your bank before traveling to ensure your credit or debit card will work in Thailand and that you won't encounter any issues with security or fraud alerts.

- **Avoid Currency Exchange at ATMs**: Many ATMs in tourist areas may offer the option to withdraw foreign currencies such as US dollars or euros. However, this is usually not the most cost-effective option. When withdrawing from ATMs in Thailand, it's better to withdraw Thai Baht directly to avoid unfavorable exchange rates and fees that may come with withdrawing foreign currencies.

4. How Much Cash Should You Bring?

While ATMs are available throughout Thailand, it's wise to have some cash on hand when you first arrive, especially if you're traveling to more rural areas or islands where ATMs may be less accessible. How much cash to bring depends on the length of your stay, your itinerary, and your spending habits.

- **For Urban Areas**: In Bangkok, Chiang Mai, Phuket, and other major cities, you can rely heavily on ATMs and credit/debit cards for most purchases. For convenience, consider bringing enough cash to cover initial expenses like transportation, food, and tips, but ATMs will take care of the rest.

- **For Rural or Remote Areas**: In more rural areas, particularly in smaller towns or islands, ATMs may be scarce, and businesses may prefer cash payments. In such cases, it's advisable to bring more cash, especially when traveling to areas without reliable banking infrastructure.

- **Estimated Daily Expenses**: A reasonable daily budget for a tourist can vary greatly depending on the style of travel. A budget traveler may spend around **500-1,000 baht** per day, while a mid-range traveler might budget between **1,500-3,000 baht** per day for accommodation, meals, and activities. For higher-end travelers, a daily budget of **5,000 baht or more** may be necessary, especially if you plan on staying in luxury hotels or dining at fine restaurants.

5. Security and Safety Tips for Handling Cash

While Thailand is generally safe for tourists, it's always important to be cautious when handling cash and managing your finances:

- **Use Hotel Safes**: When you're not using your cash or valuables, store them in your hotel room safe or a secure place. Carry only what you need for the day to minimize the risk of losing large sums of money.
- **Avoid Flashing Cash**: When walking around in busy areas, avoid displaying large amounts of cash or expensive items. This can help you avoid becoming a target for pickpockets.
- **ATM Safety**: Always use ATMs located in well-lit, busy areas. Avoid withdrawing large sums of

money late at night or from ATMs that appear to be in isolated or poorly maintained areas.

Managing your currency and banking needs in Thailand is straightforward with a bit of preparation. Understanding the exchange options available, utilizing ATMs for easy access to Thai Baht, and being aware of local banking fees will ensure you have the funds you need throughout your trip. By using a mix of cash and cards and remaining vigilant about security, you can focus on enjoying the many wonderful experiences Thailand has to offer without worrying about financial concerns.

2.3 Transportation within Thailand: Local Travel Options

When traveling within Thailand, there are a variety of local transportation options available to suit different budgets and preferences. Whether you're exploring the bustling streets of Bangkok, navigating the rural countryside, or hopping between islands, understanding the different methods of transportation will ensure you get around efficiently and comfortably.

1. Public Transportation in Bangkok

Bangkok, the capital of Thailand, is a sprawling metropolis known for its heavy traffic. However, it offers several modes of public transportation that can help you navigate the city with ease:

- **BTS Skytrain**: The **BTS Skytrain** is one of the most efficient and popular ways to get around Bangkok. This elevated train system has two main lines, the **Sukhumvit Line** and the **Silom Line**, connecting major areas such as **Siam Square**, **Chong Nonsi**, and **Mo Chit**. The Skytrain avoids Bangkok's notorious traffic jams and provides quick access to popular tourist spots, shopping districts, and business hubs. Tickets are relatively inexpensive, and you can either buy single tickets or purchase a **Rabbit Card** for easier payment on multiple trips.

- **MRT (Metro)**: The **MRT** (Mass Rapid Transit) is an underground subway system that complements the Skytrain network, covering other key areas of Bangkok, including **Chatuchak Market**, **Sukhumvit**, and **Silom**. Similar to the Skytrain, the MRT is an efficient way to travel long distances quickly, especially for areas not covered by the Skytrain. MRT stations are well-marked, and signage is available in English for ease of use.

- **Buses**: Bangkok also has an extensive bus system, with both air-conditioned and non-air-conditioned buses operating throughout the city. Buses are a more affordable option, but they can be slower due to traffic congestion. There are various types of buses, and fares are typically very inexpensive. While this is a budget-friendly option, it can be a bit confusing for tourists, as many bus routes do not have English signage. Using a bus app or Google Maps is highly recommended for first-time users.

- **Tuk-Tuks**: A quintessential Thai experience, **tuk-tuks** are small, motorized rickshaws that can be hailed from the streets. They are ideal for short trips within the city, especially when navigating through narrow lanes or when you're in a hurry. However, tuk-tuks are often more expensive than taxis, and the fare should always be negotiated in advance. Be sure to agree on a price before starting the journey, as tuk-tuk drivers may sometimes charge inflated fares to tourists.

- **Motorbike Taxis**: In Bangkok, **motorbike taxis** are a quick way to get through heavy traffic. These motorcycles are available at designated stands and can take you to your destination swiftly. While it's an inexpensive and fast option, it can be risky due to the chaotic traffic, so it's advisable to wear a helmet and only use this mode of transport for short distances. Motorbike taxis are most commonly used for solo travel, as they are not suitable for groups or larger luggage.

2. Taxis and Ride-Hailing Apps

- **Taxis**: Taxis are abundant in major cities like Bangkok, Chiang Mai, and Phuket. They are generally inexpensive, but it's important to ensure the driver uses the meter. If the driver insists on a fixed price, it's usually a sign that the fare is inflated, and you should either negotiate or look for another taxi. Taxis in Thailand are usually marked with a **bright pink, green, or yellow color** and have a **"Taxi Meter" sign** on the roof. Most taxis are clean, safe, and air-conditioned.

- **Ride-Hailing Apps (Grab)**: **Grab** is Thailand's most popular ride-hailing app, similar to Uber. It's available in Bangkok, Chiang Mai, Phuket, and several other cities. Grab offers a variety of services, including **GrabCar** (private cars), **GrabTaxi** (traditional taxis), and **GrabBike** (motorcycle taxis). The app is easy to use, and fares are typically fixed, which helps avoid overcharging. Grab also provides a safe option for booking rides with English-speaking drivers, and you can track your route in real-time.

3. Trains and Long-Distance Travel

- **State Railway of Thailand (SRT)**: The **SRT** is the country's main rail network, providing long-distance travel between Bangkok and major cities such as **Chiang Mai**, **Ayutthaya**,

Sukhothai, and **Hua Hin**. The train system is an affordable option, with various classes ranging from basic third-class seats to air-conditioned first-class sleepers. For longer trips, such as those to Chiang Mai or southern Thailand, the sleeper train is a popular choice. Trains are relatively comfortable, but they can be slow, especially for routes outside of Bangkok.

- **Express Trains**: For faster travel, there are express trains that run between major cities like Bangkok, Chiang Mai, and Surat Thani (for Koh Samui and other southern islands). These trains typically have better amenities and can be a convenient way to cover longer distances while enjoying scenic views. Train tickets can be purchased online or at train stations, and it's often a good idea to book in advance, especially during holidays or peak tourist seasons.

4. Boats and Ferries

- **Chao Phraya River Boats (Bangkok)**: In Bangkok, the **Chao Phraya River** serves as an essential transportation route for both locals and tourists. The river boats operate on several routes, providing an affordable and scenic way to travel. The **Express Boats** are a popular choice for tourists, offering a quick way to reach landmarks like the **Grand Palace, Wat Arun,** and **Asiatique**. Tickets are inexpensive and can be purchased at piers. There are also **private boats** and **charter boats** available for more personalized travel along the river.

- **Ferries and Boats to Islands**: For island-hopping or traveling to beach destinations like **Koh Samui**, **Koh Phi Phi**, **Koh Tao**, and **Krabi**, ferries are the most common and affordable option. These boats run from the mainland to various islands, and the journey can take anywhere from 1 to 5 hours, depending on the destination. Ferries typically depart from ports in **Surat Thani**, **Krabi**, and **Phuket**. It's advisable to book ferry tickets in advance, especially during peak seasons, as they can fill up quickly.

- **Longtail Boats**: In popular coastal regions like **Krabi** and **Phuket**, **longtail boats** are iconic and often used for short trips to nearby islands or beaches. These traditional wooden boats are powered by an engine attached to a long pole, and they can be hired for private tours. While they are slightly more expensive than regular ferries, longtail boats offer a more intimate and scenic way to explore Thailand's coastal beauty.

5. Bicycles and Motorbikes

- **Bicycle Rentals**: Many cities and tourist areas in Thailand offer bicycle rentals. Bangkok, Chiang Mai, and even some coastal towns have dedicated bike lanes, making cycling a fun and eco-friendly way to explore. Renting a bicycle is relatively inexpensive, and guided bike tours are available in places like **Chiang Mai** for those who want a more organized way to see the sights.

- **Motorbike Rentals**: Renting a **motorbike** is one of the most popular ways to get around, particularly in **Chiang Mai**, **Phuket**, and **Koh Samui**. Motorbikes provide the freedom to explore at your own pace and access areas that may be harder to reach by car. Motorbike rental services are widely available, and the cost is typically around **200 to 400 baht** per day for a standard scooter. However, it's important to be cautious and aware of local driving laws, wear a helmet (which is legally required), and ensure that the motorbike is insured.

6. Domestic Flights

- **Domestic Flights**: For long distances, such as traveling from Bangkok to the southern islands (e.g., Koh Samui, Krabi) or from Bangkok to Chiang Mai, **domestic flights** are often the fastest and most convenient option. Major low-cost carriers like **AirAsia**, **Thai Lion Air**, and **Nok Air** offer frequent flights at reasonable prices. The major hubs for domestic flights are **Suvarnabhumi Airport** in Bangkok and **Chiang Mai International Airport**. Booking flights in advance can help secure better rates, especially during peak travel periods.

Thailand offers a wealth of transportation options, each suited to different needs and preferences. Whether you're exploring the bustling streets of Bangkok, traveling to remote islands, or hopping between cities, there is a mode of transport that can help you reach your destination efficiently and comfortably.

2.4 Travel Insurance: What You Need to Know

Travel insurance is an essential part of planning any trip, and it is particularly important when traveling to a destination like Thailand. While Thailand is generally a safe and welcoming country, unforeseen circumstances such as illness, accidents, flight cancellations, or loss of personal belongings can disrupt your travel plans. Having the right travel insurance can provide peace of mind and financial protection in case something goes wrong during your trip.

1. Why You Need Travel Insurance

Thailand, like any international destination, can present unique challenges that make travel insurance a wise investment. Some of the main reasons to consider purchasing travel insurance for your trip to Thailand include:

- **Medical Emergencies**: While Thailand has a strong healthcare system, especially in major cities, medical costs can be high for tourists without insurance. Travel insurance typically covers emergency medical expenses, hospital stays, surgeries, and sometimes even evacuation back to your home country if necessary. This can be particularly useful for activities like trekking, diving, or motorbike riding, which may carry a higher risk of injury.

- **Trip Cancellation or Delay**: Unexpected events such as personal illness, family emergencies, or natural disasters can lead to trip cancellations or delays. Travel insurance can reimburse you for non-refundable expenses, such as flights, accommodation, and pre-paid tours, if your trip is canceled or delayed due to unforeseen circumstances.

- **Lost or Stolen Belongings**: Traveling in a foreign country always carries the risk of losing personal belongings, whether it's through theft, lost luggage, or accidental damage. Travel insurance can help cover the cost of replacing essential items like electronics, documents, and clothing if they are lost or stolen during your trip.

- **Flight Delays and Missed Connections**: Sometimes, flights are delayed or canceled due to weather, mechanical issues, or other circumstances beyond your control. Travel insurance can provide coverage for additional costs incurred, such as accommodation, meals, and transportation, if your travel plans are interrupted.

- **Adventure and Activity Coverage**: Thailand is known for its adventure tourism, including activities like diving, hiking, rock climbing, and motorbiking. Many travel insurance policies offer coverage specifically for these high-risk activities, which can be excluded from standard policies. If you plan to engage in these types of activities, ensure that your policy covers them.

2. Types of Travel Insurance Coverage

There are several types of coverage you may want to include in your travel insurance policy, depending on your needs and the nature of your trip:

- **Medical and Emergency Assistance**: This is one of the most important types of coverage for any international traveler. It includes medical expenses for illnesses or injuries that occur while you're in Thailand. Emergency assistance can also cover medical evacuation to a hospital or back to your home country if necessary.

- **Trip Cancellation/Interruption**: This coverage protects you if you need to cancel or cut your trip short due to an unexpected event, such as illness, family emergencies, or other covered reasons. You will be reimbursed for pre-paid and non-refundable trip expenses, such as flight tickets and hotel bookings.

- **Baggage Loss/Delay**: This coverage provides compensation if your baggage is lost, damaged, or delayed. It can cover the cost of replacing necessary items like clothing and toiletries if your luggage is delayed for an extended period. If your luggage is lost or stolen, the policy can help cover the replacement of valuables and personal items.

- **Flight Delay**: If your flight is delayed or canceled, travel insurance can cover the additional expenses incurred, such as accommodation, meals, and transportation costs, until your new flight is scheduled. This is particularly useful if your delay extends overnight or significantly alters your travel schedule.

- **Personal Liability**: If you cause accidental damage to property or injure someone during your trip, personal liability coverage can protect you from financial losses due to legal claims. This is particularly important if you plan to rent a vehicle or participate in high-risk activities such as motorbiking or extreme sports.

- **Adventure Sports and Activities**: As mentioned earlier, many travelers to Thailand engage in activities like scuba diving, trekking, rock climbing, or motorcycling. Standard travel insurance policies may exclude coverage for these types of activities, so it's important to ensure that your policy specifically includes **coverage for adventure sports** or high-risk activities.

3. What to Look for in a Travel Insurance Policy

When purchasing travel insurance for your trip to Thailand, there are several important factors to consider to ensure you're getting the right coverage for your needs:

- **Medical Coverage Limits**: Check the medical coverage limits to ensure that it's sufficient for your needs. Thailand has excellent medical care in major cities like Bangkok and Chiang Mai, but if you require specialized care or evacuation, the costs can add up quickly. A policy with high medical coverage limits, ideally $100,000 or more, is a good idea for peace of mind.

- **Exclusions**: Carefully read the policy for any exclusions. Common exclusions include pre-existing medical conditions, injuries sustained while under the influence of alcohol or drugs, or participation in certain high-risk activities without additional coverage. Make sure that the activities you plan to do (such as motorbiking or scuba diving) are covered or that you've purchased additional coverage for them.

- **Emergency Assistance Hotline**: A reliable travel insurance provider will offer 24/7 emergency assistance services. This can include help with arranging emergency medical treatment, finding a local doctor, or coordinating an evacuation if necessary. Check that the insurance company provides a **24-hour emergency hotline** that is accessible from Thailand.

- **Coverage for Natural Disasters**: Thailand, especially the southern regions, can be affected by natural disasters, including floods, storms, and sometimes earthquakes. Make sure your insurance covers trip delays or cancellations due to natural events, such as hurricanes or monsoons, which may disrupt travel plans.

- **Coverage for Theft or Loss**: Ensure that your policy provides adequate coverage for stolen or lost belongings, including electronics, documents, and cash. Some policies have high deductibles or low payout limits for personal property claims, so make sure the limits are sufficient for your needs.

- **Policy Flexibility**: If you are planning an extended stay or may need to change your travel plans, look for a policy that offers flexibility. Some policies allow you to extend coverage or make changes to the policy if you decide to stay longer or change your travel dates.

4. How to Buy Travel Insurance

You can purchase travel insurance from a variety of sources, including:

- **Travel Insurance Providers**: There are many specialized travel insurance companies that offer worldwide coverage for travelers, such as **World Nomads**, **Allianz Travel Insurance**, and **Travel Guard**. You can purchase policies directly from these providers online, and some may offer customizable plans to suit your needs.

- **Online Travel Agencies**: Many travel booking websites and online travel agencies (OTAs), such as **Expedia**, **Booking.com**, and **Skyscanner**, offer travel insurance options when booking flights and accommodation. While convenient, it's important to compare the policies offered by these agencies with specialized travel insurance providers to ensure you're getting the best coverage.

- **Credit Card Travel Insurance**: Some premium credit cards offer travel insurance as a benefit when you book travel using the card. This insurance may cover trip cancellations, lost luggage, or medical emergencies. However, be aware that credit card insurance may have limitations, such as lower coverage limits, and may not cover certain activities like adventure sports. Always check the details of the policy before relying on it for your trip.

- **Travel Agents**: Many travel agents can help you purchase insurance tailored to your trip. They often work with established providers and can guide you through the options available. However, it's important to compare their offerings with other providers to ensure you're getting the best deal.

5. How Much Does Travel Insurance Cost?

The cost of travel insurance depends on several factors, including your trip length, age, travel destination, the type of coverage you select, and any pre-existing medical conditions. On average, travel insurance can cost between **4% to 10%** of the total trip cost. For a two-week trip to Thailand, basic coverage might cost between **$50 and $150 USD**, while more comprehensive plans with adventure sports coverage or high medical limits could cost more.

In general, it's worth spending a little extra on a comprehensive policy, especially for longer trips, higher-risk activities, or if you're traveling with expensive equipment like cameras or laptops.

6. Claiming Travel Insurance

In the unfortunate event that you need to file a claim, most insurance companies have a straightforward process. Typically, you will need to:

- Report the incident to the appropriate local authorities (e.g., police, hospital).
- Keep all receipts, documentation, and proof of expenses related to the incident.
- Notify your insurance company as soon as possible, providing all necessary documentation.
- Submit a claim form, which you can usually do online or through an app.

It's important to keep a copy of all your travel insurance policy documents and emergency contact information with you while traveling in case of any incidents.

Travel insurance for Thailand is a wise investment that can protect you against unexpected situations, from medical emergencies to lost luggage. By understanding the different types of coverage available and selecting the right policy, you can ensure peace of mind throughout your trip and focus on enjoying all that Thailand has to offer.

Chapter 3: Exploring Thailand's Major Cities

3.1 Bangkok: The Vibrant Capital

Bangkok, Thailand's bustling capital, is a city that never sleeps. Known for its vibrant street life, ornate temples, modern skyscrapers, and chaotic traffic, Bangkok offers a unique blend of the old and the new. From historical landmarks to world-class shopping malls, this dynamic metropolis is a must-see destination for any traveler.

1. Overview of Bangkok

Bangkok, often referred to as the "City of Angels" (Krung Thep in Thai), is the largest city in Thailand and the political, cultural, and economic center of the country. With a population exceeding 8 million people, Bangkok is a melting pot of Thai culture and international influences. The city's energy is palpable, with its mix of traditional markets, modern malls, street food vendors, high-end restaurants, and vibrant nightlife.

The city is located in the central plains of Thailand, and it has become a global hub for business, finance, tourism, and entertainment. Bangkok is also an important transport gateway for Southeast Asia, with its international airport, **Suvarnabhumi Airport (BKK)**, being one of the busiest in the world.

2. Must-See Attractions in Bangkok

- **The Grand Palace and Wat Phra Kaew**: The **Grand Palace** is an iconic landmark of Thailand, once serving as the residence of the Thai kings. The palace complex is a stunning example of Thai architecture, with intricately designed buildings and impressive murals. Within the Grand Palace grounds is **Wat Phra Kaew**, the Temple of the Emerald Buddha, which houses Thailand's most revered Buddha statue. The ornate details and spiritual atmosphere make this a must-visit spot for any traveler.

- **Wat Arun (Temple of Dawn)**: Located on the banks of the Chao Phraya River, **Wat Arun** is one of Bangkok's most famous landmarks. Its towering spires, which are covered in colorful porcelain and seashells, rise dramatically above the city. Visitors can climb part of the temple for stunning views of the river and the city. It's particularly beautiful at sunrise or sunset, making it a favorite spot for photography.

- **Wat Pho (Temple of the Reclining Buddha)**: Just a short walk from the Grand Palace, **Wat Pho** is home to the famous **Reclining Buddha**, a giant gold-plated statue that measures 46 meters long. The temple is also known as the birthplace of traditional Thai massage, and visitors can enjoy a relaxing massage at the temple's massage school.

- **Chao Phraya River and Boat Tours**: The **Chao Phraya River** is central to Bangkok's identity and is often referred to as the "lifeblood" of the city. The river provides access to many of Bangkok's key attractions and offers visitors a scenic way to explore the city. Taking a boat tour along the river will allow you to see temples, markets, and residential areas, and enjoy the skyline views of the city. The **Chao Phraya Express Boat** is a convenient way to travel to key spots like **Asiatique**, **Wat Arun**, and **The Grand Palace**.

- **Chatuchak Weekend Market**: A visit to **Chatuchak** (or **JJ Market**) is essential for anyone interested in experiencing Bangkok's local culture and shopping scene. Spanning over 35 acres, Chatuchak is one of the largest markets in the world, with more than 8,000 stalls offering everything from clothing and accessories to antiques, art, and street food. Whether you're looking for souvenirs or unique local items, Chatuchak has something for everyone.

- **Siam Square and Shopping Malls**: Bangkok is a shopping paradise, and **Siam Square** is the heart of the city's shopping district. It is home to several upscale malls such as **Siam Paragon**, **MBK Center**, and **CentralWorld**, offering everything from high-end luxury brands to affordable local goods. **Siam Center** and **Siam Discovery** are also great for contemporary fashion and lifestyle stores. Shopping here is a must, especially for those interested in Thai fashion or electronics.

3. Exploring Bangkok's Local Culture

- **Street Food**: No visit to Bangkok is complete without experiencing its world-famous street food. From **Pad Thai** (stir-fried noodles) to **som tam** (green papaya salad), **mango sticky rice**, and **satay skewers**, Bangkok's street food scene is as diverse as it is delicious. Street food vendors are scattered throughout the city, but some of the best areas to indulge are around **Khao San Road, Chinatown (Yaowarat)**, and the **Sukhumvit** area.

- **Chinatown (Yaowarat)**: **Chinatown** in Bangkok is one of the most vibrant and culturally rich areas in the city. With its maze of narrow streets filled with food vendors, traditional shops, and Chinese temples, Chinatown offers a unique glimpse into the city's multicultural identity. Explore the bustling markets, sample Chinese-Thai fusion dishes, and visit the impressive **Wat Mangkon Kamalawat** temple.

- **Khao San Road**: Known as the "backpacker hub" of Bangkok, **Khao San Road** is famous for its lively atmosphere, budget accommodation, and vibrant nightlife. During the day, the street is filled with street food vendors, markets, and souvenir shops. By night, it becomes a party zone, with bars and clubs catering to both locals and tourists. Khao San Road is also home to many budget hostels, making it a popular base for travelers.

4. Getting Around Bangkok

- **BTS Skytrain**: The **BTS Skytrain** is one of the fastest and most convenient ways to get around Bangkok. It connects major areas, including **Siam**, **Sukhumvit**, and **Silom**, and avoids the heavy traffic that often plagues the streets. The trains are clean, air-conditioned, and easy to use, with signs in both Thai and English. A **Rabbit Card** can be used for multiple rides, making it a convenient payment option for frequent travelers.

- **MRT (Metro)**: Bangkok's **MRT** is another excellent way to navigate the city. The metro connects key areas such as **Sukhumvit**, **Silom**, and **Chatuchak Market**, and provides a smooth and efficient travel experience. It's especially useful for travelers heading to destinations not served by the Skytrain.

- **Taxis**: Taxis are widely available in Bangkok, and they are a convenient option for short trips or if you're traveling with luggage. Always make sure the driver uses the meter to avoid being overcharged. In busy traffic, it might be faster to take a tuk-tuk or use the **Grab** ride-hailing app.

- **Tuk-Tuks**: **Tuk-tuks** are a popular form of transport for short trips within Bangkok. While they are fun and iconic, they can be more expensive than taxis. Always agree on the fare before getting in to avoid misunderstandings.

- **River Boats**: The **Chao Phraya River** is another great way to get around Bangkok. The **Chao Phraya Express Boat** connects many of the city's key attractions along the river, and it offers both a convenient and scenic way to travel. For tourists, taking a boat ride is often faster than navigating through traffic.

5. Nightlife in Bangkok

- **Rooftop Bars**: Bangkok is home to some of the best rooftop bars in the world. With stunning views of the city skyline, these bars provide the perfect atmosphere for a drink at sunset. Popular spots include **Sky Bar** at **Lebua State Tower**,

Octave at the **Marriott Hotel Sukhumvit**, and **Mahanakhon SkyBar** in the **King Power Mahanakhon Tower**.

- **Nightclubs and Bars**: Bangkok's nightlife caters to every taste, from lively nightclubs to laid-back jazz bars. The **Royal City Avenue (RCA)** area is famous for its nightclubs, where you can dance the night away to electronic, pop, or hip-hop music. For a more relaxed atmosphere, visit one of Bangkok's many cocktail bars or enjoy some live music at a jazz bar like **Saxophone Pub** or **The Bamboo Bar**.

- **Night Markets**: Bangkok's night markets, such as the **Asiatique Riverfront Market**, **Talad Rot Fai (Train Night Market)**, and **Siam Night Market**, offer a unique shopping experience after dark. These markets feature everything from clothes and accessories to street food and antiques, with a lively ambiance that makes them perfect for evening strolls.

Bangkok's blend of historical landmarks, modern attractions, and rich cultural experiences makes it a city that offers something for every traveler. Whether you are interested in temples, shopping, dining, or vibrant nightlife, Bangkok will provide you with an unforgettable experience.

3.2 Chiang Mai: A Cultural Escape

Chiang Mai, located in the mountainous region of northern Thailand, offers a more relaxed and culturally rich alternative to the bustling capital, Bangkok. Known as the "Rose of the North," Chiang Mai is a city that seamlessly blends ancient traditions with modern influences. Its historic temples, serene landscapes, and laid-back vibe make it one of Thailand's most appealing destinations, offering a deep dive into the country's culture, history, and natural beauty.

1. Overview of Chiang Mai

Chiang Mai, founded in 1296 as the capital of the Lanna Kingdom, is one of Thailand's oldest cities. Surrounded by lush mountains and scenic countryside, the city has preserved much of its cultural heritage while embracing modern development. The city is known for its relaxed atmosphere, friendly locals, and vibrant arts and crafts scene. Chiang Mai is also a major hub for adventure activities like trekking, zip-lining, and exploring hill-tribe villages, making it an ideal destination for nature lovers and culture seekers alike.

Unlike Bangkok, which can feel overwhelming with its busy streets, Chiang Mai offers a more tranquil experience with slower-paced traffic and a more intimate vibe. The Old City, with its historic temples and narrow lanes, contrasts beautifully with the newer, more modern areas filled with cafes, markets, and boutique hotels.

2. Must-See Attractions in Chiang Mai

- **Wat Phra That Doi Suthep**: Arguably the most iconic attraction in Chiang Mai, **Wat Phra That Doi Suthep** is a mountain temple located about 15 kilometers from the city center. It sits on the slopes of **Doi Suthep Mountain**, offering spectacular views of Chiang Mai below. The temple is one of the most sacred in northern Thailand, housing a relic of the Buddha. To reach the temple, visitors can take a steep climb up 309 steps or opt for a cable car ride. The golden chedi (stupa) at the top, surrounded by intricate designs and lush greenery, is a spiritual and architectural highlight. The temple is especially stunning during sunrise or sunset when the surrounding hills are bathed in a golden glow.

- **Old City Temples**: Chiang Mai's Old City is home to many historic temples that reflect the city's long-standing Buddhist traditions. **Wat Chedi Luang** is one of the most significant temples, known for its towering, partially ruined chedi that dates back to the 14th century. Originally, it housed the Emerald Buddha, Thailand's most revered Buddha statue, before it was moved to Bangkok. **Wat Phra Singh**, another prominent temple, is known for its beautiful Lanna-style architecture and the revered Phra Singh Buddha. As you explore the Old City, you'll also encounter smaller, lesser-known temples that offer a peaceful and reflective atmosphere.

- **Chiang Mai Night Bazaar**: The **Night Bazaar** is one of the city's best-known shopping experiences. It is a vibrant market that stretches along **Chang Klan Road**, offering a variety of goods ranging from handcrafted souvenirs, jewelry, clothing, and antiques to local street food. The market is particularly lively in the evenings, with street performers adding to the atmosphere. The Night Bazaar is a great place to buy unique local products, such as **silver jewelry**, **Thai textiles**, and **wooden carvings**.

- **Wat Umong (The Tunnel Temple)**: Situated in the foothills of **Doi Suthep**, **Wat Umong** is a unique, serene temple built into the side of a mountain, known for its underground tunnels that monks use for meditation. The temple dates back to the 14th century and is located within a lush forest, making it an ideal spot for quiet reflection. The temple grounds are also home to a large pond where you can often spot koi fish, adding to the tranquil, spiritual atmosphere.

- **Chiang Mai Zoo and Aquarium**: For families or animal lovers, the **Chiang Mai Zoo** and **Aquarium** offer an opportunity to observe a wide variety of animals, including **pandas**, **tigers**, **elephants**, and local species like the **gibbon**.

The zoo is set against a backdrop of **Doi Suthep Mountain**, offering picturesque views while exploring the exhibits.

- **Bua Thong Waterfalls (Sticky Waterfalls)**: About an hour's drive from the city, **Bua Thong Waterfalls**, also known as the **Sticky Waterfalls**, offer a unique natural experience. The waterfall's limestone rock formations allow visitors to climb up the falls due to the sticky texture of the rocks. This natural wonder is a hidden gem, less crowded than other tourist spots, and offers a fun and adventurous way to interact with nature.

3. Cultural and Spiritual Experiences

- **Yi Peng Lantern Festival**: Chiang Mai is famous for its celebration of **Yi Peng**, the Lantern Festival, which takes place during the full moon of the 12th month of the lunar calendar (usually November). During this magical event, thousands of **khom loi** (sky lanterns) are released into the night sky, creating a mesmerizing sight. The festival is a spiritual occasion, and locals release the lanterns to symbolize the letting go of misfortune and bad luck. If you're visiting Chiang Mai during this time, it's a once-in-a-lifetime experience to witness this event.

- **Lanna Culture and Arts**: Chiang Mai is the center of **Lanna culture**, the traditional culture of the northern region of Thailand. Visitors can explore Lanna's artistic heritage at the **Chiang Mai City Arts and Cultural Centre**, which showcases the history, culture, and art of the Lanna Kingdom. You can also visit local **artisan workshops**, where skilled craftsmen produce traditional **handwoven textiles**, **pottery**, **silver jewelry**, and **wooden carvings**. Don't miss the **San Kamphaeng Handicraft Village**, where you can observe artisans at work and purchase handmade goods.

- **Traditional Thai Massage and Spa**: Chiang Mai is an excellent place to experience traditional **Thai massage** and spa treatments. Many spas in the city offer relaxing and rejuvenating treatments, which often incorporate herbs, oils, and ancient Thai techniques. Whether you opt for a gentle foot massage or a full-body therapeutic session, it's a perfect way to unwind after a day of exploring the city.

4. Adventure and Nature in Chiang Mai

- **Trekking and Hill Tribe Villages**: Chiang Mai is surrounded by mountains, making it a popular destination for trekking. You can explore the lush countryside and visit local **hill tribe villages**, such as the **Karen**, **Hmong**, and **Lahu** tribes. Treks vary in difficulty, from easy walks to challenging multi-day hikes. Many tours offer homestay experiences in the villages, allowing travelers to interact with the tribes and learn about their traditions and lifestyles.

- **Elephant Sanctuaries**: Chiang Mai is home to several ethical elephant sanctuaries where you can learn about these majestic animals and interact with them in a responsible and compassionate way. The **Elephant Nature Park** is one of the most well-known sanctuaries, offering visitors the chance to feed, bathe, and walk with rescued elephants. These sanctuaries focus on conservation and the rehabilitation of elephants that have been rescued from exploitation.

- **Zip-lining and Adventure Parks**: For those seeking an adrenaline rush, Chiang Mai offers several zip-lining tours and adventure parks. Companies like **Flight of the Gibbon** provide thrilling zip-lining experiences through the jungle canopy, offering a bird's-eye view of the lush forests and mountains. These activities are safe and professionally managed, making them a fun way to experience Chiang Mai's natural beauty.

5. Culinary Experiences in Chiang Mai

- **Northern Thai Cuisine**: Chiang Mai is the best place to experience **northern Thai cuisine**, which differs from the more well-known dishes of central Thailand. Northern dishes are characterized by their use of spices and herbs, as well as unique ingredients like **sticky rice** and **fermented sausages**. Be sure to try **khao soi**, a creamy curry noodle soup that is a Chiang Mai specialty, or **northern-style grilled pork (moo yang)** served with sticky rice and spicy dipping sauces. For dessert, indulge in **sticky rice with mango** or the sweet treat **kanom jeen**.

- **Cooking Classes**: Chiang Mai is known for its cooking schools, which offer hands-on classes where you can learn to prepare authentic Thai dishes. Some popular schools include **Baipai Thai Cooking School, Thai Farm Cooking School**, and **A Lot of Thai Cooking School**. These classes often start with a visit to a local market to pick out ingredients before heading back to the kitchen for a cooking lesson.

- **Sunday Walking Street Market**: If you're in Chiang Mai on a Sunday, don't miss the **Sunday Walking Street Market** on **Ratchadamnoen Road**. This market is a local favorite and is famous for its wide range of food stalls, offering everything from **grilled meat skewers** to **fresh**

fruit smoothies and traditional Thai sweets. It's also a great place to shop for local crafts and souvenirs.

Chiang Mai offers a rich tapestry of cultural, historical, and natural attractions, making it an ideal destination for travelers looking to immerse themselves in Thailand's northern traditions. Whether you're exploring ancient temples, trekking through lush mountains, or sampling northern Thai delicacies, Chiang Mai provides a fulfilling and diverse experience for all types of travelers.

3.3 Phuket: Beaches, Resorts, and Nightlife

Phuket, Thailand's largest island, is a tropical paradise known for its stunning beaches, luxurious resorts, vibrant nightlife, and diverse attractions. Located in the Andaman Sea, Phuket offers a perfect combination of natural beauty, modern amenities, and cultural experiences. Whether you're looking for a relaxing beach getaway, an adventure-filled trip, or an exciting nightlife scene, Phuket has something to offer every type of traveler.

1. Overview of Phuket

Phuket, often referred to as the "Pearl of the Andaman," is Thailand's most popular island destination. With its white sandy beaches, crystal-clear waters, and abundant resorts, it attracts millions of visitors every year. While its beaches are the main draw, Phuket also offers lush jungles, world-class spas, and a wide range of outdoor activities. The island's well-developed infrastructure ensures that travelers can enjoy both luxury and budget-friendly accommodations, dining, and entertainment options.

Phuket has a diverse landscape, from the lively and tourist-centric Patong Beach to the quieter, more serene areas like Kata Beach and Nai Harn. The island also boasts a rich cultural heritage, with historical sites, temples, and markets offering a glimpse into local life. Phuket's proximity to other islands and attractions, such as **Koh Phi Phi** and the **Phang Nga Bay**, makes it an ideal base for exploring the Andaman Sea.

2. Must-Visit Beaches in Phuket

Phuket is famous for its beaches, each offering its own charm and appeal. Whether you want to relax, swim, or participate in water sports, Phuket's beaches are a major highlight of the island.

- **Patong Beach**: Patong Beach is Phuket's most famous and bustling beach. Located on the western coast of the island, Patong is known for its vibrant nightlife, wide variety of restaurants, and an endless selection of beach clubs and bars. During the day, the beach is a hub for water sports like jet skiing, parasailing, and banana boat rides. However, it can get crowded, especially during peak season. For those who enjoy high-energy environments, Patong is the perfect beach, but it's not ideal for those seeking solitude.

- **Kata Beach**: A short distance from Patong, **Kata Beach** offers a more laid-back and family-friendly atmosphere. The beach is quieter than Patong and is known for its beautiful scenery and calm waters, making it a great place for swimming and sunbathing. The surrounding area has a mix of restaurants, cafes, and shops, with plenty of options for dining. Kata Beach also has a reputation for excellent surf conditions, especially during the monsoon season, attracting surfers from around the world.

- **Karon Beach**: Situated between Patong and Kata, **Karon Beach** is one of Phuket's longest beaches, stretching over 3 kilometers. It's less crowded than Patong but still offers a range of amenities, including restaurants, bars, and shops. The beach is perfect for those looking for a peaceful atmosphere combined with the ability to enjoy water activities like snorkeling, swimming, and beach volleyball. Karon Beach is also a great spot for evening walks, with breathtaking sunsets over the Andaman Sea.

- **Nai Harn Beach**: For those seeking tranquility and natural beauty, **Nai Harn Beach** is one of the best options on the island. Located in the southern part of Phuket, it is surrounded by lush hills and green forests, giving it a serene and peaceful vibe. Nai Harn is perfect for swimming, sunbathing, and picnicking, with clear water and soft sand. The beach is less commercialized than Patong, making it an excellent choice for travelers looking for a quiet escape.

- **Bang Tao Beach**: On the northern part of the island, **Bang Tao Beach** is known for its luxury resorts and expansive shoreline. It is one of the longest beaches on the island and offers a more refined atmosphere, with upscale beach clubs and high-end dining options. The calm waters here are perfect for swimming, and the beach is ideal for those looking for a more exclusive experience, away from the hustle and bustle of other areas like Patong.

- **Freedom Beach**: For a more private and secluded beach experience, **Freedom Beach** is a hidden gem located just south of Patong. The beach is accessible by boat or a steep, rocky path, but it rewards visitors with stunning beauty and serenity. With clear waters, soft white sand, and lush green surroundings, Freedom Beach offers a peaceful retreat far from the crowded beaches of Phuket.

3. Resorts and Accommodations

Phuket is home to a wide range of resorts, hotels, and villas, catering to every budget, from luxury stays to affordable beachfront bungalows. Whether you want an all-inclusive resort or a private villa with a pool, Phuket has plenty of options.

- **Luxury Resorts**: For a truly indulgent experience, Phuket boasts some of the world's best luxury resorts. **The Surin Phuket** on Pansea Beach offers an intimate, beachfront experience with stylish villas and a private, tranquil atmosphere. **Trisara Phuket** is another high-end resort located in a secluded area, offering private pools, stunning ocean views, and exceptional service. **Amanpuri** is one of Phuket's most prestigious resorts, nestled on the west coast with luxury villas and an exclusive spa.

- **Mid-Range Accommodations**: For those looking for mid-range options, **Holiday Inn Resort Phuket** at Patong Beach offers family-friendly amenities, with spacious rooms and beachfront access. **Kata Beach Resort & Spa** is another solid option, offering comfortable rooms, excellent dining, and direct access to the beautiful Kata Beach.

- **Budget-Friendly Options**: Budget-conscious travelers will find plenty of affordable options across Phuket. Areas like Patong and Kata have numerous guesthouses, hostels, and smaller hotels that offer great value for money. **Lub d Phuket Patong** is a popular hostel with a vibrant atmosphere, and **Phuket Graceland Resort & Spa** is a budget-friendly yet comfortable option with easy access to Patong Beach.

4. Phuket Nightlife: Bars, Clubs, and Entertainment

Phuket is known for its lively and diverse nightlife, especially in areas like Patong, which is home to some of the island's most famous bars, clubs, and entertainment venues. Whether you're looking for a relaxing cocktail by the beach, a lively nightclub experience, or a more laid-back evening, Phuket's nightlife scene caters to all tastes.

- **Bangla Road (Patong Beach)**: The heart of Phuket's nightlife, **Bangla Road** in Patong comes alive after dark. The street is lined with nightclubs, bars, go-go bars, and beer gardens, creating an electrifying atmosphere for partygoers. Popular spots include **Illuzion**, a large nightclub that attracts international DJs, and **Tiger Nightclub**, known for its vibrant neon lighting and themed parties. For a more laid-back experience, visit one of the many beach clubs, such as **Catch Beach Club** on Bang Tao Beach, which offers a relaxed vibe with music, cocktails, and a beautiful beachfront setting.

- **Beach Clubs and Lounges**: For those who prefer a more relaxed night out, **Xana Beach Club** at **Angsana Laguna Phuket** offers a chic and elegant setting with an infinity pool, great cocktails, and a lively ambiance. **Baba Beach Club** in Nai Harn is another upscale beach club where visitors can enjoy a sunset drink and dance under the stars.

- **Go-Go Bars and Cabarets**: Phuket also has its share of adult-oriented entertainment, particularly in Patong. **Simon Cabaret**, one of Thailand's most famous cabarets, offers an extravagant show featuring glamorous costumes and stunning performances. If you're looking for something more adventurous, the go-go bars around Bangla Road are known for their lively shows and exuberant energy.

- **Sunset Bars**: For a more relaxed vibe, many bars in Phuket offer stunning sunset views. **The Surface Bar** at **Phuket Marina** is a chic lounge offering a great spot to watch the sunset over the water while enjoying a drink. **The 360 Bar** on **Kata Beach** is another fantastic venue to sip cocktails while watching the sun dip below the horizon.

5. Activities and Attractions in Phuket

Beyond the beaches and nightlife, Phuket offers plenty of activities and attractions for visitors of all interests.

- **Phi Phi Islands**: A day trip to the **Phi Phi Islands** is one of the most popular excursions from Phuket. These islands are known for their dramatic cliffs, crystal-clear waters, and stunning beaches. You can take a boat tour, go snorkeling, or visit **Maya Bay**, which was made famous by the film *The Beach*.

- **Phang Nga Bay**: Famous for its limestone karsts and emerald-green waters, **Phang Nga Bay** is another must-see destination near Phuket. Visitors can explore the bay by kayak, visit **James Bond Island** (featured in the film *The Man with the Golden Gun*), or simply take a boat tour through this scenic and serene area.

- **Water Sports and Adventure**: Phuket is a prime destination for water sports like **scuba diving**, **snorkeling, windsurfing**, and **kite surfing**. Areas like Kata Beach, Patong, and Kamala Beach offer equipment rentals, guided tours, and diving schools for all levels. Additionally, you can go zip-lining, ATV riding, or explore **Phuket**

Elephant Sanctuary for a chance to learn about Thailand's wildlife conservation efforts.

Phuket offers an ideal blend of relaxation, adventure, and entertainment. Whether you're soaking up the sun on the beach, indulging in luxury, or exploring vibrant nightlife, the island provides a diverse experience for all kinds of travelers.

3.4 Pattaya: Fun and Adventure for All Ages

Pattaya, located on the eastern Gulf coast of Thailand, is one of the country's most popular resort cities, known for its vibrant nightlife, entertainment, and wide array of activities for both adults and families. While Pattaya has long been associated with its lively party scene, it has undergone a transformation in recent years, offering a more diverse range of attractions, including family-friendly activities, outdoor adventures, and cultural experiences. Pattaya is now a destination that caters to all kinds of travelers, whether you're looking to relax on the beach, enjoy thrilling activities, or explore cultural and natural attractions.

1. Overview of Pattaya

Pattaya is just a two-hour drive from Bangkok, making it an easily accessible destination for both local and international tourists. The city has grown from a quiet fishing village into a major tourist hotspot, and it offers a mix of bustling urban life and tranquil escapes. Pattaya is known for its long beaches, which line the coastline, and the vibrant **Walking Street**, famous for its nightlife, bars, and clubs. However, the city has much more to offer beyond the party scene, with everything from family-friendly water parks and animal attractions to cultural landmarks and scenic nature spots.

Whether you're visiting for a weekend getaway or a longer stay, Pattaya is packed with fun, adventure, and entertainment for all ages. Here's an exploration of the highlights of Pattaya, offering something for every type of traveler.

2. Must-Visit Attractions in Pattaya

- **Walking Street**: **Walking Street** is Pattaya's most famous attraction, and it's the center of the city's nightlife. As the sun sets, the street comes alive with neon lights, music, and crowds. It is filled with nightclubs, bars, go-go clubs, restaurants, and street performers. While Walking Street is primarily known for its adult entertainment, it is also home to several family-friendly restaurants, shopping opportunities, and live music venues. If you're visiting with family, it's best to explore Walking Street earlier in the evening, as the area can get quite crowded and rowdy later at night.

- **Pattaya Beach**: The city's main beach, **Pattaya Beach**, is ideal for those looking to relax by the sea. With a wide variety of water sports available, such as jet skiing, parasailing, and banana boat rides, the beach offers something for everyone. While the beach can be busy, there are plenty of beach chairs and umbrellas for rent, and vendors provide snacks and drinks to keep you refreshed. If you're looking for a quieter beach experience, nearby **Jomtien Beach** offers a more laid-back atmosphere with fewer crowds.

- **Sanctuary of Truth**: The **Sanctuary of Truth** is an awe-inspiring wooden temple located on the northern coast of Pattaya. The temple is entirely constructed from teak wood and features intricate carvings depicting Hindu and Buddhist mythological figures. Visitors can explore the temple's beautiful architecture and learn about Thailand's spiritual and cultural traditions. The Sanctuary of Truth is also an active construction project, with artisans working on the structure, making it a fascinating place to visit.

- **Pattaya Floating Market**: The **Pattaya Floating Market** is a unique cultural experience where visitors can shop for local products, crafts, and traditional Thai food from boats that float on the canals. The market is divided into four sections, representing the central, northern, northeastern, and southern regions of Thailand. The market offers a great way to sample regional delicacies, such as **som tam** (papaya salad), **pad thai**, and tropical fruits, while enjoying traditional Thai music and performances.

- **Nong Nooch Tropical Garden**: For nature lovers, **Nong Nooch Tropical Garden** is a stunning botanical garden just outside Pattaya. The expansive grounds feature beautifully landscaped gardens, including a French garden, a cactus garden, and an orchid garden. Visitors can stroll through the gardens, watch cultural performances, or visit the on-site elephant show. The garden is also home to a large collection of exotic plants and flowers, making it a peaceful and picturesque escape from the hustle and bustle of the city.

3. Family-Friendly Activities in Pattaya

- **Cartoon Network Amazone Waterpark**: Pattaya is home to **Cartoon Network Amazone**, a massive water park themed around the popular Cartoon Network characters. The park features water slides, wave pools, and lazy rivers, with themed areas dedicated to shows like **The Amazing World of Gumball**, **Adventure Time**, and **Ben 10**. With attractions suitable for both young children and adults, Cartoon Network Amazone is a fun way to cool off and enjoy a day of thrills with the whole family.

- **Pattaya Dolphin World**: **Pattaya Dolphin World** is an exciting marine park where visitors can enjoy shows featuring dolphins and sea lions. The park also offers the opportunity to swim with dolphins and learn about marine life in an interactive environment. The dolphin shows are a big hit with families, especially children, making it a great way to spend a fun and educational day.

- **Underwater World Pattaya**: For those interested in marine life, **Underwater World Pattaya** offers an immersive experience with an impressive aquarium filled with a wide variety of sea creatures, including sharks, stingrays, and sea turtles. The highlight of the attraction is the 100-meter-long tunnel that allows visitors to walk through the aquarium and watch marine animals swim overhead. It's a fantastic experience for both children and adults, offering a chance to learn about the diverse marine life in Thailand.

- **Khao Kheow Open Zoo**: Located a short drive from Pattaya, **Khao Kheow Open Zoo** is one of Thailand's largest zoos and home to more than 8,000 animals. The zoo offers a more natural setting for animals, with open-air enclosures that mimic their natural habitats. Visitors can see a variety of animals, including tigers, elephants, giraffes, and orangutans. The zoo also offers animal shows, night safaris, and a chance to interact with some animals in safe and controlled environments, making it an ideal family outing.

4. Adventure Activities in Pattaya

- **Skydiving**: For thrill-seekers, **skydiving** is one of the most exciting ways to experience Pattaya. The **Pattaya Skydiving Center** offers tandem skydives where visitors can jump out of an airplane and soar above the island, taking in panoramic views of the Gulf of Thailand and the surrounding coastline. With professional instructors, it's a safe and exhilarating adventure for those looking for an adrenaline rush.

- **Bungee Jumping**: Pattaya is one of the few places in Thailand where you can experience **bungee jumping**. Located in the **Pattaya Bungy Jump**, visitors can leap from a 60-meter platform overlooking a picturesque lake. For thrill-seekers, this is a must-do activity to push your limits and enjoy a unique view of Pattaya from above.

- **ATV and Dirt Bike Tours**: For those interested in outdoor adventure, Pattaya offers ATV (all-terrain vehicle) and dirt bike tours through the rugged terrain and jungle surroundings. You can explore off-road trails, ride through dirt paths, and navigate hills and forests on an exhilarating ride. Several tour operators in Pattaya offer guided ATV tours for different skill levels, making it an exciting way to experience the natural beauty of the area.

- **Go-Kart Racing**: **Easy Kart Pattaya** is one of the best go-karting venues in Thailand, offering a thrilling racing experience for both beginners and experienced drivers. Located near Jomtien Beach, the track is set in a scenic area and provides a fun and competitive environment for families or groups of friends to race against each other.

5. Pattaya Nightlife: Fun After Dark

Pattaya's nightlife is one of its most famous attractions, drawing visitors from all over the world. Whether you're looking for lively bars, live music, or a more relaxed evening, Pattaya has plenty to offer.

- **Walking Street**: As mentioned earlier, **Walking Street** is the epicenter of Pattaya's nightlife. It comes alive after dark, with clubs, bars, and go-go bars lining the street. It's an iconic area for adult entertainment and partying, with neon lights, loud music, and plenty of street food.

- **Beach Clubs and Bars**: For a more laid-back evening, Pattaya offers several beach clubs and bars along the coastline. **The Roof Sky Bar & Restaurant** offers panoramic views of the beach, while **Horizon Bar** at the Hilton Pattaya provides a stylish setting for sunset cocktails. Many of these venues offer live music, making for a relaxed yet lively atmosphere as you unwind with drinks by the beach.

- **Cabaret Shows**: Pattaya is famous for its glamorous **cabaret shows**, particularly the **Tiffany's Show** and **Alcazar Cabaret**. These colorful and vibrant performances feature dazzling costumes, music, and dance routines. They are a must-see for visitors looking for an entertaining, lighthearted night out.

Pattaya is a diverse city that offers a little something for everyone, whether you're visiting as a family, a couple, or with friends. With its range of beaches, adventure activities, cultural experiences, and exciting nightlife, Pattaya ensures that every traveler has an unforgettable time in Thailand.

Chapter 4: Unique Experiences and Activities

4.1 Thailand's Beautiful Islands: Exploring Krabi, Koh Samui, and Koh Phi Phi

Thailand is home to some of the most stunning islands in the world, offering a perfect blend of natural beauty, crystal-clear waters, white sandy beaches, and vibrant local culture. Each island has its own charm and unique characteristics, attracting different types of travelers. Whether you're looking for relaxation, adventure, or cultural experiences, islands like **Krabi**, **Koh Samui**, and **Koh Phi Phi** have it all. In this section, we will dive deeper into what makes these islands such incredible destinations and what unique experiences they offer.

1. Krabi: Adventure and Serenity in Nature

Krabi, located on the Andaman Sea in southern Thailand, is known for its dramatic limestone cliffs, clear turquoise waters, and secluded beaches. The province is a gateway to some of Thailand's most picturesque islands, including **Railay Beach** and **Ko Lanta**, but Krabi itself has much to offer in terms of outdoor adventure, cultural experiences, and natural beauty.

- **Railay Beach**: One of Krabi's most famous attractions, **Railay Beach**, is accessible only by boat, adding to its allure and making it feel like a remote paradise. This stunning area is known for its towering limestone cliffs, making it a hotspot for rock climbers. The beach offers crystal-clear water and soft sand, perfect for swimming or sunbathing. The nearby **Phra Nang Cave Beach** is home to caves and a revered princess cave filled with offerings to the spirits, adding a spiritual element to the scenic beauty.

- **Phi Phi Islands**: Krabi is often the starting point for excursions to the **Phi Phi Islands**, which are about 45 minutes by boat. **Koh Phi Phi Don** is the largest island, offering stunning viewpoints, lively beaches, and vibrant nightlife, while **Koh Phi Phi Leh** is famous for **Maya Bay**, made famous by the movie *The Beach*. Although **Maya Bay** has been closed to tourists for environmental recovery, the Phi Phi islands still offer spectacular snorkeling, diving, and boat tours.

- **Ao Nang**: The main tourist hub in Krabi, **Ao Nang**, is a bustling beach town with a range of accommodations, dining options, and shopping opportunities. While Ao Nang is more developed than Railay, it is still a fantastic base for exploring the nearby islands. You can also take a boat trip to secluded beaches like **Ao Thalane** for kayaking through mangroves or hike up to the **Ao Nang Viewpoint** for panoramic views of the coastline.

- **Tiger Cave Temple**: For those seeking cultural experiences, **Wat Tham Sua (Tiger Cave Temple)** is a must-visit. Located a short drive from Krabi town, this temple is perched on a hilltop, offering panoramic views of the surrounding countryside. To reach the top, visitors must climb over 1,200 steps, but the effort is worth it for the breathtaking views and the sense of spiritual fulfillment.

- **Emerald Pool and Hot Springs**: Krabi is also home to some natural hot springs and unique swimming spots. The **Emerald Pool** is a natural hot spring located in **Klong Thom** and is known for its clear, turquoise waters surrounded by lush jungle. Nearby, **Tha Pom Klong Song Nam** offers a serene and refreshing walking tour through a mangrove forest, where you can see the unique "twin streams" that run through the area.

2. Koh Samui: Luxury, Beaches, and Wellness

Koh Samui, located in the Gulf of Thailand, is one of Thailand's most famous islands, offering a mix of luxury resorts, pristine beaches, wellness retreats, and lively entertainment. The island's tropical climate, palm-fringed beaches, and rich cultural heritage make it an appealing destination for travelers seeking both relaxation and adventure.

- **Chaweng Beach**: **Chaweng Beach** is Koh Samui's most popular beach, known for its vibrant nightlife, shopping, and dining. This beach is perfect for those who want to enjoy the sun, surf, and vibrant atmosphere. By day, you can relax on the soft sand and swim in the clear waters, while in the evening, the area transforms into a lively scene with beach clubs, restaurants, and bars offering live music and cocktails.

- **Lamai Beach**: A more tranquil alternative to Chaweng, **Lamai Beach** offers a relaxed vibe with beautiful sunsets and calmer waters. This beach is great for swimming, kayaking, or simply unwinding in the peaceful surroundings. The beach is dotted with restaurants and resorts that offer a mix of budget and luxury options.

- **Big Buddha Temple**: One of the island's most iconic landmarks, **Wat Phra Yai**, also known as the **Big Buddha Temple**, is located on a small island connected by a causeway. The 12-meter tall golden Buddha statue is an impressive sight and is surrounded by smaller statues and shrines. Visitors can also enjoy panoramic views of the island from the temple grounds.

- **Ang Thong National Marine Park**: A must-do excursion from Koh Samui, **Ang Thong National Marine Park** is a stunning archipelago of 42 islands located about an hour by boat from Koh Samui. The park is famous for its limestone mountains, hidden lagoons, and incredible snorkeling opportunities. Activities like kayaking, hiking, and boat tours are popular in the park, with highlights including the **Emerald Lake** on **Koh Mae Ko**, a saltwater lake surrounded by dramatic cliffs.

- **Wellness Retreats and Spas**: Koh Samui is renowned for its wellness offerings, from yoga retreats to luxurious spas. Many resorts offer wellness programs that include spa treatments, yoga, meditation, detox programs, and healthy cuisine. **Kamalaya Wellness Sanctuary** and **Absolute Sanctuary** are two of the most well-known wellness centers on the island, offering a range of treatments aimed at rejuvenating the body and mind.

- **Secret Buddha Garden**: Located in the center of the island, the **Secret Buddha Garden** is an idyllic spot to explore. Nestled in the hills, the garden is filled with statues, shrines, and lush greenery, providing a peaceful and spiritual escape. The views from the garden are stunning, and the area's tranquility contrasts with the bustling coastal regions of the island.

3. Koh Phi Phi: Iconic Beauty and Adventure

The **Phi Phi Islands**, located in the Andaman Sea, are among the most famous and photographed islands in Thailand, thanks to their dramatic cliffs, clear waters, and vibrant coral reefs. Koh Phi Phi consists of several islands, the largest being **Phi Phi Don** and the smaller **Phi Phi Leh**, which is famous for its role in the movie *The Beach*. The Phi Phi Islands are a paradise for nature lovers, adventure seekers, and anyone looking to experience breathtaking landscapes.

- **Maya Bay**: **Maya Bay** on **Koh Phi Phi Leh** is undoubtedly the most famous spot in the Phi Phi Islands, thanks to the 2000 film *The Beach*, starring Leonardo DiCaprio. The bay, surrounded by towering cliffs, was closed to tourists for environmental recovery but is set to reopen in the future. Despite its closure, you can still visit the surrounding islands and enjoy their beauty. The nearby **Loh Samah Bay** and **Pileh Lagoon** are known for their crystal-clear water and stunning scenery.

- **Snorkeling and Scuba Diving**: The Phi Phi Islands are renowned for their vibrant marine life, making them a prime destination for snorkeling and scuba diving. Popular spots like **Shark**

Point, **Bamboo Island**, and **Hin Klang** are filled with colorful coral reefs, tropical fish, and even blacktip reef sharks. Several diving shops on the islands offer guided tours and diving courses for all levels, making it an excellent spot to explore underwater.

- **Hiking to Phi Phi Viewpoint**: For those who enjoy a bit of adventure, hiking to the **Phi Phi Viewpoint** is a must. The hike takes you up to a vantage point where you can see panoramic views of the entire island, including the famous crescent-shaped bay of **Ton Sai** Beach and the surrounding islands. The viewpoint is especially beautiful at sunrise or sunset, offering stunning photo opportunities.

- **Viking Cave**: The **Viking Cave** on **Phi Phi Leh** is another notable attraction. The cave is famous for its ancient paintings, which are believed to depict Viking ships, although the origins of the artwork are unclear. The cave is also used for the collection of bird nests, which are used in the famous bird's nest soup, a delicacy in Thai cuisine.

- **Kayaking and Island Hopping**: Exploring the Phi Phi Islands by kayak is one of the best ways to see the stunning coastline. Paddle through hidden caves, lagoons, and secluded beaches, or hop between islands, enjoying the peaceful surroundings and crystal-clear water. Kayaking tours are popular and often include stops at other nearby islands such as **Koh Bida Nok** and **Koh Yung**.

Thailand's islands offer a diverse range of experiences, from the peaceful serenity of Koh Samui's wellness retreats to the adrenaline-filled adventures on the Phi Phi Islands. Whether you're looking to relax on pristine beaches, dive into vibrant underwater worlds, or explore unique cultural landmarks, islands like **Krabi**, **Koh Samui**, and **Koh Phi Phi** will provide an unforgettable experience. Each of these destinations brings its own unique appeal, making them essential stops for anyone looking to experience the best of Thailand's island paradise.

4.2 Adventure and Sports: Hiking, Diving, and More

Thailand is renowned not only for its stunning landscapes and beautiful beaches but also for its wealth of outdoor adventure opportunities. Whether you're looking for thrilling water sports, challenging hikes through jungles and mountains, or the chance to explore underwater ecosystems, Thailand has something for every type of adventure enthusiast. From the highlands in the north to the crystal-clear waters in the south, here are some of the top adventure and sports activities to experience in Thailand.

1. Hiking and Trekking in Thailand

Thailand offers a wide variety of hiking and trekking opportunities, from jungle trails to mountain summits. For those looking to explore the country's diverse landscapes on foot, these trails provide an immersive experience in nature, culture, and wildlife.

- **Chiang Mai and Northern Thailand**: Chiang Mai is the gateway to some of the best trekking routes in Thailand. The region's cool climate and mountainous terrain make it ideal for hiking. One of the most popular treks is to **Doi Inthanon**, the highest peak in Thailand at 2,565 meters. Hikers can explore a range of trails that wind through dense forests, visit waterfalls, and reach the summit for breathtaking views. The region is also home to various **hill tribe villages**, where trekkers can interact with the local communities and learn about their traditional lifestyles.

- **Pai and the Pai Canyon**: For a more laid-back yet scenic hiking experience, head to **Pai**, a small town in northern Thailand. Surrounded by hills, waterfalls, and rice paddies, Pai offers a number of trails with spectacular views. **Pai Canyon**, located just outside the town, offers a short but rewarding hike along narrow ridges with panoramic views of the surrounding valleys. Visitors can also explore **Tham Lod Cave** or take a trek to visit **the hot springs** in the area.

- **Khao Yai National Park**: As Thailand's first UNESCO-listed national park, **Khao Yai** is a popular destination for trekking and wildlife spotting. With diverse ecosystems ranging from tropical rainforest to grassland, Khao Yai offers numerous trekking trails suitable for different experience levels. Hikers may encounter elephants, gibbons, and a wide variety of bird species along their journey. Trails like **Haew Suwat Waterfall Trail** and **Pha Kluai Mai Waterfall Trail** are popular for their scenic beauty and wildlife opportunities.

- **Erawan National Park**: Located in **Kanchanaburi, Erawan National Park** is famous for its stunning **seven-tiered waterfall**. The hiking trail to the falls takes you through lush jungle, where you can swim in natural pools beneath the waterfalls. The hike is relatively easy, making it perfect for families or casual hikers, and the beauty of the waterfalls makes it one of the most popular trekking destinations in Thailand.

- **Phu Kradueng National Park**: A challenging but rewarding hike, **Phu Kradueng** in northeastern Thailand offers a unique trekking experience. Hikers ascend to a plateau and spend the night in a campsite, where they can explore the stunning landscapes of the park, including waterfalls, cliffs, and valleys. The park is known for its biodiversity, and hiking here gives visitors a chance to see rare flora and fauna.

2. Scuba Diving and Snorkeling

Thailand is one of the best places in the world to explore underwater ecosystems. The country's clear waters, vibrant coral reefs, and rich marine life make it a top destination for scuba diving and snorkeling. Whether you are a seasoned diver or a beginner, Thailand offers a range of diving sites to suit all levels.

- **Similan Islands**: Located in the Andaman Sea, the **Similan Islands** are one of Thailand's most famous diving spots. Known for their clear waters, diverse marine life, and vibrant coral reefs, the Similan Islands offer some of the best diving in the world. The islands are home to giant manta rays, whale sharks, sea turtles, and a variety of tropical fish. The waters are perfect for both beginner and advanced divers, with dive sites ranging from shallow reefs to deep walls and underwater pinnacles.

- **Koh Tao**: Known as the "diving mecca" of Thailand, **Koh Tao** is a small island off the coast of **Koh Samui** that attracts divers from all over the world. Koh Tao offers some of the best-value dive courses, including **PADI Open Water Certification**, and features numerous dive sites like **Chumphon Pinnacle**, where divers can spot large schools of fish, and **Shark Bay**, where blacktip reef sharks can often be seen. The island is ideal for both beginners and experienced divers, with clear water and a variety of dive sites ranging from shallow coral gardens to deeper reefs.

- **Koh Phi Phi**: The **Phi Phi Islands** are another world-class diving destination. Known for their dramatic cliffs and crystal-clear waters, the Phi Phi Islands offer a range of dive sites, including **Maya Bay** and **Hin Klang**. These sites are known for vibrant coral reefs, deep drop-offs, and an abundance of marine life, including parrotfish, moray eels, and rays. Phi Phi's diving conditions are excellent, especially during the dry season, and it's a great place for both diving enthusiasts and beginners.

- **Koh Lanta**: Koh Lanta, located near Krabi, is a quieter alternative to the more famous dive sites. It's home to **Koh Haa**, a group of islands with stunning underwater caves and deep water swim-throughs. The area is known for its peaceful ambiance and less crowded dive sites, making it perfect for those who want to explore without the tourist rush. The coral reefs around Koh Lanta are rich with marine life, and the island is a great place to get away from the hustle and bustle of more popular destinations.

- **Snorkeling in Phang Nga Bay**: While Phang Nga Bay is famous for its dramatic limestone cliffs and caves, it also offers fantastic snorkeling opportunities. Kayaking through the bay's caves can bring you to hidden lagoons with colorful fish, and nearby islands like **James Bond Island** provide excellent snorkeling spots. The water is calm and shallow, making it perfect for beginner snorkelers.

- **The Andaman Sea**: If you're in southern Thailand, the Andaman Sea offers a range of stunning snorkeling opportunities. Areas like **Krabi**, **Koh Lanta**, and **Phuket** are home to vibrant coral reefs teeming with fish, sea turtles, and marine life. The shallow waters in these regions make them great for snorkeling, and many operators offer boat trips to remote islands and reefs.

3. Water Sports and Beach Activities

Beyond diving and snorkeling, Thailand offers a wide range of water sports and beach activities, perfect for adrenaline seekers and those who enjoy spending time on the water.

- **Jet Skiing**: Jet skiing is one of the most popular water sports in Thailand, especially on islands like **Koh Samui, Phuket,** and **Krabi**. Many beaches offer jet ski rentals, allowing you to race across the water and enjoy the thrill of speed. However, it's important to make sure you rent from a reputable company to avoid scams or overcharging.

- **Parasailing**: Parasailing is another popular activity on Thailand's beaches. Many beaches, including **Patong Beach** in Phuket and **Chaweng Beach** in Koh Samui, offer parasailing experiences where you can soar high above the water and take in stunning views of the coastline. It's an exhilarating activity that combines adventure with sightseeing.

- **Stand-Up Paddleboarding (SUP)**: Stand-up paddleboarding is growing in popularity in Thailand, especially in calmer waters like those found in **Koh Samui, Koh Lanta,** and **Koh Tao**. Paddleboarding is a relaxing way to explore the coastline, providing an excellent workout and a chance to enjoy the tranquility of the water. It's perfect for both beginners and seasoned paddlers.

- **Wakeboarding**: For thrill-seekers, wakeboarding is another great water sport to try in Thailand. Wakeboarding is available in **Koh Samui, Koh**

Phangan, and **Phuket**, with numerous operators offering lessons and rentals. You can try it on the calm waters of the island's lakes, or take to the sea for a more intense experience.

- **Windsurfing and Kitesurfing**: Thailand's calm winds and warm waters make it an excellent destination for windsurfing and kitesurfing. **Hua Hin** is particularly popular for kitesurfing, and **Koh Samui** offers opportunities for windsurfing, especially during the monsoon season when the winds are at their best.

4. Rock Climbing

Thailand is a renowned destination for rock climbers, with some of the best limestone cliffs in the world. The country offers a variety of climbing opportunities, from beginner-friendly crags to challenging overhangs.

- **Railay Beach (Krabi)**: **Railay Beach** is famous for its dramatic limestone cliffs, which attract climbers from around the world. The cliffs range in difficulty, with many routes suitable for beginners and intermediate climbers. Popular spots include **Phra Nang Cave Beach** and **Ton Sai Beach**, both of which offer stunning views and incredible climbing experiences. Railay Beach also offers professional climbing schools where you can take lessons and improve your skills.

- **Koh Phi Phi**: Known for its stunning scenery and crystal-clear waters, **Koh Phi Phi** is also a great destination for rock climbing. The island offers several climbing routes along its limestone cliffs, with incredible views of the ocean below. Whether you're a beginner or an experienced climber, Phi Phi provides a range of climbing options.

- **Chiang Mai**: For climbers looking to explore northern Thailand, **Chiang Mai** offers several excellent climbing locations, including the popular **Crazy Horse Buttress**. The area is known for its sport climbing routes, with a range of difficulties and stunning views of the surrounding countryside.

Thailand's adventure sports scene offers something for everyone, from the tranquil waters of Koh Samui to the high cliffs of Krabi. Whether you're into diving, rock climbing, hiking, or water sports, you'll find a variety of thrilling activities to make your trip to Thailand unforgettable.

4.3 Thai Cuisine: A Culinary Journey

Thai cuisine is one of the most beloved and flavorful in the world, known for its harmonious balance of spicy, sweet, sour, salty, and bitter flavors. With an emphasis on fresh ingredients, aromatic herbs, and bold seasonings, Thai food offers a sensory journey that takes you through a vibrant palette of tastes. Whether you're enjoying a simple street food dish or a refined meal at a luxury restaurant, Thai cuisine has something to delight every palate. In this section, we'll explore some of the key elements of Thai cuisine, the must-try dishes, and the experiences that will take you deeper into Thailand's culinary culture.

1. Key Ingredients in Thai Cooking

Before diving into the dishes themselves, it's important to understand the essential ingredients that form the backbone of Thai cuisine. Thai food is characterized by its use of fresh herbs and spices, which contribute to its distinctive flavors.

- **Lemongrass**: A fragrant herb used in Thai soups, curries, and marinades. It adds a citrusy, slightly sweet flavor and is often used in Thai dishes like **Tom Yum** and **Tom Kha Gai** (coconut soup).

- **Galangal**: A relative of ginger, galangal has a sharper, more peppery flavor and is frequently used in curries and soups like **Green Curry** and **Tom Yum**. Its aromatic qualities are essential to many Thai dishes.

- **Kaffir Lime Leaves**: These leaves have a strong citrus aroma and are used to impart a zesty flavor to broths, curries, and stir-fries. They are often torn or sliced and added towards the end of cooking.

- **Thai Basil**: With a slightly peppery, anise-like flavor, Thai basil is used in many stir-fries and curries. The **holy basil** variety is often used in spicy dishes like **Pad Krapow Moo** (stir-fried pork with basil).

- **Chilies**: Thai cuisine is known for its bold use of chilies, which provide both heat and depth of flavor. **Bird's eye chilies** are the most commonly used and are found in many traditional dishes. Thai food can be incredibly spicy, but the level of heat can often be adjusted to your preference.

- **Fish Sauce (Nam Pla)**: One of the key elements in Thai cooking, fish sauce is made from fermented fish and provides a salty, umami flavor to dishes. It's used in nearly everything, from curries to dipping sauces and salads.

- **Coconut Milk**: Coconut milk adds a rich, creamy texture to many Thai soups and curries, particularly in southern Thai cuisine. It balances out the spiciness of many dishes and is used in famous dishes like **Massaman Curry** and **Tom**

Kha Gai.

- **Tamarind**: The tangy, sour flavor of tamarind is used in many Thai sauces and pastes, contributing to the distinctive flavor of dishes like **Pad Thai** and **Tom Yum Soup**.

2. Must-Try Dishes in Thai Cuisine

Thai food is incredibly diverse, with each region offering its own specialties and signature dishes. Below are some of the must-try dishes that capture the essence of Thailand's culinary richness.

- **Pad Thai**: One of the most iconic dishes of Thai cuisine, **Pad Thai** is a stir-fried noodle dish typically made with rice noodles, shrimp or chicken, tofu, eggs, bean sprouts, peanuts, and lime. It's often served with a side of chili flakes and sugar for adjusting the flavor. This savory-sweet dish is balanced with the freshness of lime and the crunchiness of peanuts.

- **Tom Yum Soup**: A spicy and sour soup made with shrimp (or chicken), mushrooms, lemongrass, kaffir lime leaves, and galangal, **Tom Yum** is one of Thailand's most famous soups. The balance of tangy lime, spicy chilies, and the richness of fish sauce makes it a flavor-packed starter or meal.

- **Green Curry (Gaeng Keow Wan)**: Known for its rich, aromatic flavors, **Green Curry** is made from a paste of green chilies, lemongrass, garlic, and coconut milk, and it's typically cooked with chicken, beef, or tofu. It is a fragrant and flavorful curry, which combines spiciness with sweetness from the coconut milk.

- **Massaman Curry**: A mild, fragrant curry with Indian and Muslim influences, **Massaman Curry** is typically made with beef or chicken, potatoes, peanuts, and coconut milk. The curry is flavored with cinnamon, cardamom, cloves, and tamarind, giving it a rich and comforting taste.

- **Som Tum (Green Papaya Salad)**: A refreshing and spicy salad, **Som Tum** is made from shredded green papaya, chilies, garlic, tomatoes, peanuts, and dried shrimp, all tossed together in a mortar and pestle with fish sauce, lime, and sugar. It's a perfect balance of spicy, sour, salty, and sweet.

- **Pad Krapow Moo (Basil Stir-Fry)**: A simple but flavorful stir-fry made with minced pork (or chicken), garlic, chilies, and **holy basil**, **Pad Krapow Moo** is often served with rice and a fried egg on top. The dish is known for its bold, aromatic flavors, and it's one of the most beloved street foods in Thailand.

- **Khao Pad (Fried Rice)**: A quintessential Thai dish, **Khao Pad** is fried rice typically made with shrimp, chicken, or pork, along with vegetables, eggs, and soy sauce. This dish is often served with fresh cucumber slices and a wedge of lime.

- **Mango Sticky Rice (Khao Niew Mamuang)**: For dessert, **Mango Sticky Rice** is a classic Thai treat, made with sweet sticky rice, fresh mango, and coconut milk. The dish is simple but incredibly satisfying, with a perfect balance of sweetness and creaminess.

3. Regional Specialties

Different regions of Thailand have distinct culinary traditions, with each area using local ingredients and flavors to create unique dishes.

- **Northern Thailand**: The cuisine of **Northern Thailand** is known for its milder flavors, with a focus on sticky rice, sausages, and stews. **Khao Soi**, a curried noodle soup with crispy noodles on top, is a regional favorite. The north is also known for its **Lanna cuisine**, with dishes like **Nam Prik Ong** (a spicy tomato-based dip served with vegetables) and **Sai Ua** (a spicy herbal sausage).

- **Isaan (Northeastern Thailand)**: **Isaan cuisine** is known for its bold and fiery flavors, with an emphasis on sourness and spiciness. **Som Tum** (green papaya salad) is the most famous dish from this region, but **Larb** (a minced meat salad) and **Sticky Rice** (often served with grilled meats) are also staples of Isaan food. The cuisine often incorporates fermented fish and local herbs to create a complex flavor profile.

- **Southern Thailand**: **Southern Thai cuisine** is famous for its use of coconut milk, turmeric, and fresh seafood. The food is known for its rich, bold flavors, and many dishes are quite spicy. **Khao Yum** (spicy rice salad) and **Gaeng Tai Pla** (fish curry) are some of the region's most famous dishes. Southern Thailand also has a strong Muslim influence, which is reflected in dishes like **Roti** (a type of flatbread) and **Massaman Curry**.

- **Central Thailand**: The heart of Thailand's culinary scene, **Central Thailand** is home to the country's most well-known dishes, including **Pad Thai**, **Tom Yum Soup**, and **Green Curry**. Central Thai cuisine balances a variety of flavors, with both spicy and mild options available. Street food in Bangkok and surrounding areas often includes skewered meats, noodle soups, and sweet treats like **Coconut Ice Cream**.

4. Thai Street Food Culture

Street food is an essential part of Thai food culture, and it offers an affordable way to enjoy authentic local flavors. In every major city and town, from Bangkok to Chiang Mai and Phuket, street food vendors line the streets, offering an array of freshly prepared dishes. Whether it's **Satay (grilled skewers)**, **Thai-style Crepes (Roti)**, or **Goi Tod (fried snacks)**, street food provides a convenient and delicious way to sample traditional Thai cuisine. Markets such as **Chatuchak in Bangkok**, **Sunday Walking Street in Chiang Mai**, and the **Phuket Night Market** are great places to explore and enjoy street food.

Many vendors specialize in specific dishes, and you can often find food stalls offering **Khao Man Gai (chicken rice)**, **Moo Ping (grilled pork skewers)**, and **Sweets** like **Thong Yod** (sweet golden egg yolk dessert). Eating at a street food stall is not only an opportunity to enjoy the flavors of Thailand, but it's also a way to immerse yourself in the local culture and experience the social side of dining.

5. Cooking Classes: Learn to Make Thai Food

If you want to take your Thai food experience to the next level, consider taking a **Thai cooking class**. Many schools and local chefs offer hands-on classes where you can learn how to prepare traditional dishes. These classes often start with a tour of a local market, where you'll select ingredients and learn about the different spices and herbs used in Thai cuisine. Afterward, you'll head to the kitchen to prepare dishes like **Pad Thai**, **Tom Yum Soup**, and **Green Curry**. Cooking classes are available in major tourist destinations like **Bangkok**, **Chiang Mai**, and **Koh Samui**, and they provide an immersive way to deepen your understanding of Thai food.

6. Thai Beverage and Desserts

- **Thai Iced Tea**: One of Thailand's most popular drinks, **Thai iced tea** is a sweet and refreshing beverage made with strongly brewed tea, condensed milk, and sugar, served over ice. It's perfect for cooling off on a hot day.

- **Thai Iced Coffee**: Similar to Thai iced tea, **Thai iced coffee** is made with strong coffee, condensed milk, and sugar, offering a rich and sweet flavor.

- **Coconut Water**: Fresh **coconut water** is a refreshing, naturally sweet drink available throughout Thailand. You'll often find street vendors selling chilled coconuts, which they'll open for you to drink straight from the coconut.

- **Khao Niew Mamuang (Mango Sticky Rice)**: Thailand's most famous dessert, **Mango Sticky Rice**, is a simple yet delightful treat made with sticky rice, coconut milk, and ripe mango. The balance of sweetness from the coconut milk and the fresh mango makes it a perfect finish to any meal.

Thai cuisine offers a wide variety of flavors, ingredients, and experiences, making it an essential part of any trip to Thailand. Whether you're dining at a street food stall, indulging in a luxury restaurant, or trying your hand at cooking, Thai food is sure to leave a lasting impression.

4.4 Festivals and Events: Must-See Thai Celebrations

Thailand is a country steeped in rich cultural traditions, and its festivals are a vibrant reflection of its history, religion, and customs. From Buddhist holidays to lively national celebrations, Thai festivals are an immersive experience for travelers, offering a unique opportunity to witness local culture in action. These festivals showcase the spirit of Thai hospitality, the importance of family, and the connection to spirituality. Whether you visit during traditional religious observances or exuberant celebrations, the following are some of the must-see festivals and events that bring Thailand to life.

1. Songkran Festival (Thai New Year)

When: April 13–15
Where: Nationwide, especially in **Bangkok, Chiang Mai, Phuket,** and **Ayutthaya**

Songkran is Thailand's most famous and widely celebrated festival, marking the traditional Thai New Year. The festival is a time for families to reunite, pay respects to elders, and clean their homes in preparation for the new year. But it's the **water fights** that have made Songkran famous worldwide. Streets are transformed into water battlefields as locals and tourists alike arm themselves with water pistols and buckets to splash each other in good fun. The festival lasts for several days and includes cultural ceremonies such as visiting temples, making offerings to monks, and performing traditional rituals to honor ancestors.

The water festivities are symbolic, as they represent the cleansing of bad luck and the welcoming of good fortune. **Chiang Mai** is particularly famous for its large-scale Songkran celebrations, with the old city center becoming a water-fight zone, while **Bangkok's Silom Road** also sees massive crowds joining in the fun. In addition to the water battles, you'll find traditional processions, live music, and cultural performances. **Songkran** is an exhilarating experience that showcases both the playful and spiritual sides of Thai culture.

2. Loy Krathong Festival

When: November (on the full moon of the 12th lunar month)
Where: Nationwide, with major celebrations in **Chiang Mai**, **Bangkok**, **Sukhothai**, and **Ayutthaya**

Loy Krathong is one of Thailand's most beautiful and spiritually significant festivals. The name "Loy Krathong" translates to "float a krathong," referring to the small, decorated floating baskets made of banana leaves that are launched into rivers, lakes, and other bodies of water. The act of releasing the krathong is symbolic of letting go of past grievances, bad luck, and misfortune, and it is believed to bring good fortune in the future.

The festival is celebrated on the full moon night of the 12th month of the lunar calendar, and it coincides with the end of the rainy season. While the central tradition involves floating the krathong, the festival also features spectacular light displays, traditional Thai dancing, fireworks, and the release of lanterns (known as **khom loi**) into the sky. In **Chiang Mai**, you can also witness the spectacular Yi Peng Festival, where thousands of glowing lanterns are released into the night sky, creating a magical sight.

In **Bangkok**, the Chao Phraya River becomes the focal point of Loy Krathong celebrations, with locals and visitors alike gathering along the riverbanks to release their krathongs. The event is one of Thailand's most picturesque festivals, offering a truly unforgettable experience.

3. Yi Peng Lantern Festival

When: November (same time as Loy Krathong)
Where: Chiang Mai

The **Yi Peng Lantern Festival** takes place in northern Thailand, particularly in **Chiang Mai**, and it's one of the most visually stunning events in the country. This festival, held around the same time as Loy Krathong, is known for the release of thousands of lanterns into the sky, creating a breathtaking spectacle. The lanterns, or **khom loi**, symbolize the release of sins and bad luck, and their ascent into the sky is seen as a form of prayer for good health and happiness.

During Yi Peng, you can also enjoy traditional Thai cultural performances, such as folk music, dance, and street parades. The highlight of the festival is when the sky is illuminated with thousands of floating lanterns, creating an ethereal atmosphere that has become iconic in photographs. Many temples in **Chiang Mai** also hold special ceremonies where monks light lanterns as part of religious observances, adding a spiritual dimension to the celebrations.

Yi Peng is a magical and serene festival that is best experienced in Chiang Mai, where the combination of floating lanterns, cultural rituals, and natural beauty creates an unforgettable atmosphere.

4. Chinese New Year

When: January or February (dates vary based on the lunar calendar)
 Where: Bangkok, Chiang Mai, Yaowarat (Chinatown)

Thailand is home to a large Chinese population, and **Chinese New Year** is celebrated with vibrant festivities throughout the country. The celebrations are particularly grand in **Bangkok's Chinatown (Yaowarat)**, where the streets come alive with dragon dances, lion dances, fireworks, and traditional performances. You'll find colorful decorations, red envelopes (symbolizing good luck), and offerings to ancestors at temples during this time.

During Chinese New Year, markets are filled with delicious Chinese street food, including **dumplings**, **noodles**, and **sweet treats** like **bak kua** (grilled dried pork). The entire city of **Bangkok** becomes immersed in the spirit of the festival, with parades and fireworks lighting up the night sky. Chinese New Year is a celebration of family, prosperity, and the ushering in of a new year with good fortune, and it offers a glimpse into the fusion of Thai and Chinese cultures.

5. Vegetarian Festival (Tesagan Gin Je)

When: September or October (dates vary based on the lunar calendar)
 Where: Phuket, Bangkok, Krabi

The **Vegetarian Festival**, also known as **Tesagan Gin Je**, is a unique and somewhat extreme celebration that takes place in several parts of Thailand, with **Phuket** being the epicenter of the festival. The festival is observed by Chinese communities and is centered around spiritual cleansing and self-purification, with participants following a vegetarian or vegan diet for the duration of the event.

What sets this festival apart is the **rituals of self-mortification** performed by devotees. Participants engage in acts of physical endurance, such as walking on hot coals, piercing their bodies with sharp objects, and performing other rituals that are believed to purify the body and bring good fortune. The festival is marked by colorful processions, where people march through the streets with their bodies pierced and decorated in ceremonial attire, all while chanting and celebrating.

Despite the intense nature of the rituals, the Vegetarian Festival is also a time of community celebration. You can find a wide variety of vegetarian Thai street food, including **stir-fried tofu**, **vegetable curries**, and **mock meat** dishes, all offering a chance to taste some of the best vegetarian food Thailand has to offer.

6. Loy Krathong Yi Peng (Lantern Festival) in Sukhothai

When: November (same time as Loy Krathong and Yi Peng)
Where: **Sukhothai**

The **Sukhothai Loy Krathong** celebration is unique in that it is often regarded as the "original" birthplace of the Loy Krathong festival. Sukhothai, the ancient capital of Thailand, offers a more traditional and historical setting for this celebration, with the ruins of the old city providing a majestic backdrop for the festival's events.

The festival in Sukhothai includes the traditional releasing of **krathongs** (floating baskets) into the water, but the event also features beautiful light displays, traditional dances, and a majestic parade with royal costumes and performances. The Sukhothai celebration is often quieter and more reflective than the celebrations in Chiang Mai and Bangkok, making it perfect for those seeking a more peaceful and cultural experience.

7. King's and Queen's Birthday Celebrations

When: **King's Birthday** – July 28 (King Maha Vajiralongkorn)
Queen's Birthday – August 12 (Queen Sirikit)
Where: Nationwide

The birthdays of Thailand's monarchs are significant national holidays, celebrated with grandeur and reverence across the country. These are times when the Thai people pay tribute to the monarchy, and the streets, especially in **Bangkok**, are decorated with royal portraits, flags, and lights. On these days, special ceremonies are held at the **Grand Palace**, and public celebrations include fireworks, cultural performances, and community events.

The **Queen's Birthday** is also celebrated as **Mother's Day** in Thailand, with special events honoring the role of mothers in Thai society. People often make offerings to the royal family and attend public celebrations to show respect for the monarchy.

Thailand's festivals and events provide an opportunity to witness the country's vibrant traditions, unique culture, and deep spiritual roots. From water festivals and lantern celebrations to royal birthdays and vegetarian rituals, these events offer a rich, immersive experience for anyone visiting Thailand during these times.

Chapter 5: Accommodation in Thailand

5.1 Hotels: Luxury, Mid-Range, and Budget Options

Thailand offers a wide range of accommodation options that cater to all types of travelers. Whether you're looking for a luxurious resort with private beaches, a budget-friendly guesthouse in a bustling city, or a mid-range hotel offering comfort and convenience, Thailand's accommodation options are diverse and plentiful. In this section, we'll explore the different categories of hotels, including luxury, mid-range, and budget options, to help you choose the best place to stay based on your preferences, needs, and budget.

1. Luxury Hotels and Resorts

Thailand is renowned for its luxury accommodations, offering world-class service, breathtaking views, and exclusive experiences. Whether located on the beach, in the mountains, or within vibrant cities, luxury hotels in Thailand promise exceptional amenities, fine dining, and impeccable service. Many luxury resorts also offer specialized wellness programs, private villas, and tailored experiences to make your stay unforgettable.

- **Four Seasons Resort Koh Samui**: Situated on the beautiful island of **Koh Samui**, the **Four Seasons Resort** offers luxury villas and private beachfront retreats. The resort features an award-winning spa, fine dining with locally sourced ingredients, and activities such as Thai cooking classes, yoga, and water sports. The resort's beautiful hilltop location offers stunning views of the Gulf of Thailand, making it a perfect place to unwind in absolute luxury.

- **The Peninsula Bangkok**: Located along the Chao Phraya River in **Bangkok**, the **Peninsula Bangkok** offers unparalleled views of the city's skyline and river. The hotel combines traditional Thai design with modern luxury, offering spacious rooms, a renowned spa, and multiple dining options. Guests can enjoy the hotel's infinity pool overlooking the river and take a private boat shuttle to nearby attractions, including the Grand Palace and Wat Arun.

- **Amanpuri, Phuket**: Known for its exclusivity, **Amanpuri** on **Phuket** is one of Thailand's most luxurious resorts. Situated on the west coast of the island, this resort features elegant pavilions and beachfront villas that offer the ultimate privacy and tranquility. The resort is surrounded by lush tropical gardens and pristine beaches, and guests can indulge in a wide range of activities such as spa treatments, sailing, and gourmet dining.

- **Mandarin Oriental, Chiang Mai**: For those seeking a luxurious experience in northern Thailand, **Mandarin Oriental** in **Chiang Mai** provides a serene retreat with riverfront views, traditional Lanna-inspired architecture, and world-class amenities. The hotel features an outdoor pool, an award-winning spa, and exceptional dining options, offering a perfect balance of luxury and cultural charm.

- **Banyan Tree Phuket**: This luxurious resort offers a private oasis with all-villa accommodations, some with private pools, nestled in tropical gardens. The **Banyan Tree Phuket** is known for its exceptional spa, which offers traditional Thai healing therapies, and its fine dining experiences. The resort also provides exclusive activities like private yacht charters and golf at the nearby Laguna Phuket Golf Club.

2. Mid-Range Hotels

Mid-range hotels in Thailand provide a balance of comfort, convenience, and affordability. These accommodations typically offer more spacious rooms, modern amenities, and good service at a price that's more accessible than luxury resorts. Mid-range hotels are perfect for travelers looking for comfort without breaking the bank.

- **Holiday Inn Resort Phuket**: Located near Patong Beach, the **Holiday Inn Resort Phuket** is an excellent choice for families and couples. The hotel features a large pool, spacious rooms with contemporary decor, and multiple dining options. It's within walking distance of Patong's shopping and entertainment options but offers a quieter, more relaxed atmosphere than other nearby resorts.

- **Novotel Bangkok Sukhumvit 20**: Situated in the heart of Bangkok's vibrant **Sukhumvit** district, the **Novotel Bangkok Sukhumvit 20** offers stylish accommodations with easy access to shopping, dining, and entertainment. The hotel features spacious rooms, a rooftop pool with views of the city skyline, and a variety of dining options. It's a great option for travelers looking for modern amenities and convenience.

- **The Surin Phuket**: Located on the secluded Pansea Beach, the **Surin Phuket** offers a more relaxed atmosphere than the bustling Patong area while still providing easy access to the island's attractions. The hotel features charming cottages, some with direct beach access, an infinity pool, and excellent restaurants. It's an ideal choice for those seeking a balance of relaxation and adventure.

- **Centara Grand at CentralWorld, Bangkok**: Situated in the heart of **Bangkok**, the **Centara Grand** offers easy access to shopping malls, including the **CentralWorld Mall**, one of Southeast Asia's largest shopping complexes. The hotel provides comfortable rooms, excellent dining options, a large outdoor pool, and a spa. With its central location, it's perfect for those who want to explore Bangkok's vibrant city life.

- **Kata Beach Resort & Spa, Phuket**: Located on the more peaceful **Kata Beach**, this resort offers comfortable rooms, a spa, and a range of recreational activities like snorkeling and beach volleyball. It's an ideal choice for travelers seeking a more relaxed beach experience while still having access to the amenities and activities available in Phuket.

3. Budget Hotels and Guesthouses

For travelers on a tighter budget, Thailand offers a wide variety of budget hotels and guesthouses that provide basic accommodations at a fraction of the cost of mid-range and luxury options. These accommodations offer comfort, convenience, and the chance to immerse yourself in local culture while saving money.

- **Khao San Road (Bangkok)**: The famous **Khao San Road** is home to a wide range of budget accommodations, from hostels to guesthouses. Known as the backpacker hub of Bangkok, Khao San offers simple, affordable rooms that are perfect for those who want to explore the city without spending too much on lodging. **Khao San Road** is also a great place for socializing, with plenty of street food, bars, and activities for travelers.

- **Lub d Phuket Patong**: Located in Patong, **Lub d** is a popular choice for budget travelers and backpackers. It offers dormitory-style rooms and private rooms with modern amenities, a fun social atmosphere, and great facilities like a bar, pool table, and café. It's ideal for those who want to enjoy the lively atmosphere of Patong while staying in affordable, clean accommodations.

- **Green House Hostel, Chiang Mai**: **Green House Hostel** in Chiang Mai is an affordable guesthouse offering both private rooms and dormitory beds. The hostel is centrally located, just a short walk from the Old City and popular attractions like the **Chiang Mai Night Bazaar**. It offers basic but comfortable accommodations with helpful staff and a friendly atmosphere, making it a great option for backpackers and budget travelers.

- **P2 Boutique Hotel, Bangkok**: For those looking to stay in a central location on a budget, **P2**

Boutique Hotel in **Siam Square** is a fantastic option. The hotel offers modern rooms with all essential amenities, including free Wi-Fi, air conditioning, and a flat-screen TV. It's within walking distance of major shopping malls like **Siam Paragon** and **MBK Center** and is a short walk from the Skytrain station, making it a convenient base for exploring Bangkok.

- **The Racha, Koh Racha Yai**: For an affordable beach resort option, **The Racha** on **Koh Racha Yai** offers budget-friendly bungalows and villas in a stunning beachside location. While it's not as luxurious as other high-end resorts, it offers basic accommodations with access to beautiful beaches, great diving, and outdoor activities.

- **Bodega Hostel, Krabi**: In **Krabi**, the **Bodega Hostel** is a popular choice for backpackers and budget travelers looking for social interaction and affordable accommodations. The hostel offers both private rooms and dormitory-style rooms, along with a communal area, bar, and organized activities, creating a fun and welcoming atmosphere for travelers.

4. Hostels and Homestays

In addition to hotels, Thailand is home to a wide range of hostels and homestays, which are often perfect for solo travelers or those looking to experience local life more intimately. Many of these accommodations offer a social environment, where you can meet fellow travelers and share experiences.

- **The Overstay, Bangkok**: This artsy, alternative hostel in **Bangkok** offers budget-friendly dorm rooms, communal spaces, and a laid-back atmosphere. It's located a bit off the beaten path, giving it a more relaxed vibe compared to the more tourist-heavy areas. It's ideal for travelers looking for something a bit different.

- **Sawasdee House, Chiang Mai**: A guesthouse in the heart of Chiang Mai's Old City, **Sawasdee House** offers a homely atmosphere with affordable rooms and friendly service. The guesthouse is conveniently located near temples, restaurants, and markets, making it easy for guests to explore the cultural sights of the city.

- **Homestays in Northern Thailand**: If you're looking for a unique cultural experience, consider staying with a **hill tribe family** in northern Thailand. Many local families offer homestays where you can learn about traditional lifestyles, customs, and cuisine. Homestays provide an immersive and authentic experience that many hotels can't match.

Thailand's diverse range of accommodation options ensures that every traveler can find a place to suit their budget and preferences. Whether you're enjoying a luxury resort in Koh Samui, staying in a charming guesthouse in Chiang Mai, or connecting with fellow backpackers at a hostel in Bangkok, Thailand's accommodations offer something for everyone.

5.2 Unique Stays: Eco-Resorts, Floating Hotels, and Villas

For travelers seeking something beyond the typical hotel experience, Thailand offers a wealth of unique accommodations that blend luxury, nature, and creativity. From eco-resorts nestled in the jungle to floating hotels on tranquil waters and private villas offering total privacy, these one-of-a-kind stays provide a more immersive and unforgettable experience. Whether you're an eco-conscious traveler, an adventure seeker, or someone in search of ultimate relaxation, Thailand's unique stays offer something for every kind of guest.

1. Eco-Resorts: Sustainable Luxury Amid Nature

Eco-resorts in Thailand offer a sustainable and environmentally friendly alternative to traditional accommodations, allowing travelers to stay in beautiful natural surroundings while minimizing their impact on the environment. These resorts focus on conservation, using local materials, renewable energy, and eco-friendly practices to create a harmony between luxury and nature.

- **Soneva Kiri, Koh Kood**: Located on the unspoiled island of **Koh Kood**, **Soneva Kiri** is a luxury eco-resort that blends stunning design with environmental consciousness. The resort uses solar power, recycles waste, and has an extensive sustainability program that includes organic farming and reef conservation. Its villas are built using local materials and offer incredible views of the ocean and surrounding jungle. Guests can enjoy outdoor experiences like kayaking, tree-top dining, and private beach picnics, all while staying in a resort that embraces sustainability.

- **The Escape Hotel, Koh Phangan**: **The Escape Hotel** on **Koh Phangan** is an eco-conscious retreat located on a hillside with panoramic views of the island. The resort features solar-powered villas, an organic vegetable garden, and sustainable building materials. Known for its tranquil atmosphere and commitment to eco-tourism, this hotel offers wellness retreats, yoga classes, and sustainable tours. Guests can explore the island's natural beauty through eco-friendly activities such as kayaking, hiking, and forest walks.

- **Khao Sok Jungle Huts, Surat Thani**: For those wanting to experience Thailand's rainforests firsthand, **Khao Sok Jungle Huts** offers eco-friendly huts set in the heart of **Khao Sok National Park**, one of the oldest rainforests in the world. The resort focuses on preserving the natural habitat while providing guests with an unforgettable experience in the wild. You can stay in treehouses, explore the jungle with expert guides, go kayaking on **Cheow Lan Lake**, or simply relax in nature's embrace. The resort also supports local wildlife conservation efforts.

- **Treehouse Villas, Koh Yao Noi**: Set in the peaceful island of **Koh Yao Noi**, **Treehouse Villas** offers sustainable, luxury treehouse accommodation that is perfect for those who want to get closer to nature. Each villa is designed to blend seamlessly into the surrounding rainforest, offering a private and secluded experience with panoramic views of **Phang Nga Bay**. The resort emphasizes sustainability with an eco-friendly approach to energy use, water conservation, and waste management. Guests can enjoy activities like kayaking, yoga, and cooking classes while experiencing the island's natural beauty.

2. Floating Hotels and Resorts: Stay on the Water

Thailand's waterways are home to some truly unique floating hotels and resorts, where guests can enjoy the serenity of living on the water. These accommodations offer a one-of-a-kind experience that allows you to be surrounded by nature while staying in a luxurious, comfortable setting.

- **Anantara Khao Lak Resort & Spa, Phang Nga Bay**: One of the most luxurious floating resorts in Thailand, the **Anantara Khao Lak** offers an exceptional experience with floating villas that overlook the stunning **Phang Nga Bay**. The resort's over-water villas feature private plunge pools, expansive terraces, and views of the bay's limestone cliffs and emerald-green waters. Guests can also enjoy private cruises, watersports, and treatments at the resort's spa, which overlooks the serene ocean. The resort is ideal for those looking to immerse themselves in both luxury and the surrounding natural beauty.

- **Koh Panyi Floating Village**: Located on **Phang Nga Bay**, **Koh Panyi** is a floating village built on stilts, home to a community of fishermen. While it's not a luxury resort, staying overnight in one of the village's local guesthouses or on floating bungalows offers a unique cultural experience. Visitors can explore the village by boat, interact with local families, and enjoy fresh seafood directly from the surrounding waters. It's an ideal destination for those interested in experiencing the traditional, sustainable way of life in a floating community.

- **Koh Samui Floating Villas**: For a private floating experience, **Koh Samui** has several floating villas and boutique resorts that offer peaceful stays right on the water. These floating villas often feature contemporary designs with glass walls, infinity pools, and luxurious bedrooms with panoramic ocean views. Some of these villas come with personal chefs, private boat tours, and the opportunity to enjoy an exclusive retreat away from the crowds.

- **Four Seasons Tented Camp Golden Triangle**: For those seeking something truly unique, **Four Seasons Tented Camp Golden Triangle** is an all-inclusive luxury experience in northern Thailand, situated along the **Ruak River** near the borders of Thailand, Myanmar, and Laos. The resort features tented accommodations on floating platforms, where you can enjoy the beautiful river views, watch elephants in the nearby sanctuaries, and enjoy activities like zip-lining, trekking, and boat tours along the river. The resort's intimate and adventurous setting offers guests a truly exceptional stay in nature.

3. Private Villas: Exclusivity and Luxury

For travelers seeking the ultimate in privacy, exclusivity, and luxury, private villas in Thailand offer an unparalleled level of comfort and service. These villas often come with private pools, direct access to the beach, personal chefs, and the ability to customize your experience to suit your needs. Perfect for honeymooners, families, or groups of friends, private villas provide a high-end experience while maintaining a sense of seclusion and intimacy.

- **Villa Shanti, Koh Samui**: Nestled on the hillside of **Koh Samui**, **Villa Shanti** is a stunning private villa that offers breathtaking views of the surrounding beaches and islands. The villa features spacious bedrooms, an infinity pool, an outdoor dining area, and a fully-equipped kitchen. Guests enjoy a high level of privacy and luxury, with a personal butler, chef, and housekeeper on hand to cater to every need. The villa's serene location and intimate setting make it perfect for a romantic getaway or a private retreat.

- **The Pavilions Phuket**: Located in the peaceful **Layan Beach** area of **Phuket**, **The Pavilions Phuket** offers a collection of luxurious, private villas with private pools and panoramic ocean views. Each villa comes with an outdoor terrace, a large infinity pool, and access to the resort's world-class amenities, including a wellness center and fine dining options. The resort is designed for guests who want to enjoy a private, exclusive experience while still having access to the island's attractions.

- **Villa Samadhi, Koh Samui**: A stunning private retreat located on the serene shores of **Koh Samui**, **Villa Samadhi** offers a luxurious escape with breathtaking views of the Gulf of Thailand. The villa features spacious living areas, a private infinity pool, and a lush garden surrounding the property. Guests can also enjoy personalized experiences such as private cooking classes, in-villa massages, and guided tours of nearby attractions.

- **Banyan Tree Private Villas, Phuket**: Located on the tranquil **Laguna Phuket**, **Banyan Tree** offers a collection of private pool villas with expansive layouts, ensuring complete privacy and luxury. Each villa is equipped with modern amenities, an outdoor jacuzzi, and personalized service. The resort's private villas are ideal for those looking for an intimate, relaxing stay with easy access to the area's exclusive golf course, spa, and dining options.

4. Unique and Themed Stays

For those seeking something truly out-of-the-ordinary, Thailand also offers unique, themed accommodations that provide a distinctive way to experience the country's culture, nature, and architecture. These stays are perfect for travelers looking for something beyond the traditional hotel or resort experience.

- **Elephant Hills, Khao Sok National Park**: For nature lovers and animal enthusiasts, **Elephant Hills** offers the chance to stay in **luxury tented camps** in the heart of **Khao Sok National Park**. This eco-friendly experience allows guests to immerse themselves in nature while enjoying comfortable accommodations with beautiful views. Visitors can participate in activities like **elephant encounters**, jungle trekking, and canoeing on the peaceful lakes.

- **The Royal Princess Tent, Sukhothai**: For a unique cultural experience, stay in **The Royal Princess Tent**, located near the ancient city of **Sukhothai**. This glamping experience offers a luxurious take on traditional camping, where guests can enjoy the beauty of Sukhothai's historical parks and UNESCO World Heritage sites while staying in elegant tented accommodations. The tents are furnished with plush bedding, and guests can take guided tours through the ancient ruins of Sukhothai and nearby villages.

- **Treepod Dining at Soneva Kiri, Koh Kood**: While not a traditional accommodation, **Soneva Kiri's Treepod Dining** experience is a unique way to dine. Guests are hoisted into a treehouse pod, where they can enjoy a multi-course meal while overlooking the pristine jungle and ocean below. This experience is perfect for couples or special occasions, offering a truly unique dining adventure in the treetops.

Thailand's unique stays offer something for everyone, from luxurious eco-resorts to floating hotels and private villas. Whether you're looking to immerse yourself in nature, experience ultimate privacy, or indulge in a one-of-a-kind adventure, Thailand's unique accommodations promise to create lasting memories.

5.3 Hostels and Guesthouses: A Backpacker's Guide

Thailand is a backpacker's paradise, with an abundance of affordable hostels and guesthouses that offer comfortable, budget-friendly accommodations. Whether you're a solo traveler, part of a group, or a first-time backpacker, staying in a hostel or guesthouse allows you to meet fellow travelers, share stories, and experience the local culture while keeping costs down. From lively party hostels to tranquil retreats in remote areas, Thailand's hostels and guesthouses cater to a wide range of tastes and travel styles.

In this guide, we'll explore some of the best hostels and guesthouses across Thailand, giving you an overview of the types of accommodation available for backpackers, tips for booking, and recommendations for the best places to stay.

1. What to Expect from Hostels and Guesthouses in Thailand

Hostels and guesthouses in Thailand vary widely in terms of style, amenities, and atmosphere. Here are some general features to expect:

- **Dormitory Rooms**: Most hostels feature dormitory-style rooms, which are typically the most budget-friendly option. Dorms often range from 4 to 16 beds, with shared bathrooms. They're ideal for solo travelers or those who want to meet others. Bunk beds are common, and many hostels offer female-only dorms for added comfort and security.

- **Private Rooms**: For those who prefer more privacy, many guesthouses and hostels offer private rooms, often at a higher cost than dormitories. These rooms can range from basic, budget-friendly options with shared bathrooms to more luxurious rooms with en-suite bathrooms.

- **Social Atmosphere**: Many hostels are designed to foster social interaction, with common areas where guests can relax, hang out, and meet fellow travelers. These areas may include lounges, kitchens, or even bars and cafés. Hostels often organize social events like pub crawls, game nights, or cooking classes to encourage mingling.

- **Free Amenities**: Hostels in Thailand often provide free amenities, such as Wi-Fi, lockers, and sometimes breakfast or coffee. Some hostels may also offer free maps, travel tips, and organized tours of nearby attractions. Budget hostels are often more basic but functional, while mid-range options might include extra comforts like air-conditioning or swimming pools.

- **Location**: Hostels and guesthouses in Thailand are generally located in tourist hotspots such as **Bangkok**, **Chiang Mai**, **Phuket**, **Koh Samui**, **Pai**, and **Krabi**. Some are in the heart of the action, close to nightlife and markets, while others are set in quieter areas or more scenic locations, offering a relaxing environment for rest and rejuvenation.

2. Popular Hostel and Guesthouse Destinations

Thailand is home to many areas that are perfect for backpackers looking to explore the country's rich culture, stunning landscapes, and vibrant social scenes. Here are some of the top destinations for backpackers and the best places to stay in each location.

Bangkok

The capital city of Thailand, **Bangkok**, is one of the most popular destinations for backpackers. With its bustling streets, vibrant nightlife, historic temples, and modern shopping malls, Bangkok is a city that never sleeps. Hostels here are diverse, offering everything from party-friendly hostels to laid-back spots for relaxation.

- **Khao San Road**: Known as the backpacker hub of Bangkok, **Khao San Road** is lined with budget-friendly guesthouses and hostels. It's the perfect area for meeting other travelers, as the street is filled with vibrant bars, street food vendors, and market stalls. Recommended hostels in this area include **The Rambuttri Village Inn & Plaza**, which is close to the action but offers a more peaceful atmosphere, and **Bodega Bangkok**, a social hostel with a lively bar and activities for guests.

- **Sukhumvit**: If you prefer a more modern and cosmopolitan atmosphere, **Sukhumvit** is a great area to stay. Hostels like **Lub d Bangkok Sukhumvit 33** offer stylish and comfortable dorms and private rooms, a large common area, and plenty of social activities. This area has excellent transportation connections to explore the rest of Bangkok.

Chiang Mai

Chiang Mai, in northern Thailand, is a top destination for backpackers due to its mix of rich history, adventure opportunities, and peaceful atmosphere. Whether you're here to visit temples, trek in the mountains, or take a cooking class, Chiang Mai has plenty of budget-friendly places to stay.

- **The Artel Chiang Mai**: Located in the Old City, **The Artel** offers both private rooms and dorms with a relaxed atmosphere. It's a great spot for travelers who want to experience the city's culture, visit temples, or explore local markets.

- **Green Tiger House**: If you're seeking a more tranquil, nature-inspired guesthouse, **Green Tiger House** offers comfortable, eco-friendly rooms and a beautiful garden setting. It's a quieter option compared to hostels near the Night Bazaar and is perfect for those who want to relax after a day of exploring.

Koh Phi Phi

Koh Phi Phi, an island paradise in southern Thailand, is known for its stunning beaches, crystal-clear waters, and vibrant party scene. Backpackers flock here for the beaches, nightlife, and iconic sights like **Maya Bay** (made famous by the movie *The Beach*).

- **The Pier 119 Hostel**: Located near the pier, **The Pier 119 Hostel** offers a relaxed atmosphere with dormitory-style rooms and private options. It's an ideal base for exploring Koh Phi Phi, and it offers affordable prices and easy access to nearby beaches and the famous nightlife.

- **Blanco Beach Bar Hostel**: Situated right on **Long Beach**, **Blanco Beach Bar Hostel** is a popular choice for party-loving backpackers. The hostel offers beachfront accommodation, social events, and a lively atmosphere with its own bar. It's perfect for those who want to enjoy the beach by day and join in the nightlife at night.

Pai

Pai, a small town nestled in the mountains of northern Thailand, is known for its bohemian atmosphere, beautiful scenery, and chilled vibe. It's a popular destination for backpackers looking to escape the hustle and bustle of city life.

- **Pai Circus School**: This fun and quirky guesthouse offers more than just a place to sleep—it offers activities like circus skills training, yoga, and communal meals. **Pai Circus School** is a social and laid-back place, perfect for those who want to meet other travelers while enjoying the natural beauty of Pai.

- **Bamboo Hut**: A charming guesthouse located in a serene area near **Pai Canyon**, **Bamboo Hut** offers affordable bungalows with lovely views of the surrounding countryside. It's a peaceful place to stay if you're looking to relax and unwind.

Koh Samui

Koh Samui, one of Thailand's most famous islands, is a great mix of luxury and laid-back vibes. For backpackers, there are plenty of budget accommodations available, many of which are located near the island's beaches and nightlife hubs.

- **The Hostel Koh Samui**: Located in **Chaweng Beach**, **The Hostel Koh Samui** is a vibrant and social place to stay. It offers dormitory rooms with a fun, party-oriented atmosphere and hosts regular events like bar crawls and karaoke nights. It's ideal for those looking to socialize and enjoy the island's lively nightlife.

- **Samui Backpacker Hotel**: For those who prefer a quieter, more relaxed stay, **Samui Backpacker Hotel** in **Maenam** provides affordable accommodations in a peaceful setting. The hotel is located near the beach and offers a laid-back atmosphere with comfortable rooms and basic amenities.

3. Tips for Booking Hostels and Guesthouses in Thailand

- **Book in Advance**: While many hostels and guesthouses in Thailand have walk-in availability, booking in advance is highly recommended, especially during peak seasons (November to February). Booking platforms like **Booking.com**, **Hostelworld**, and **Agoda** provide an easy way to find and compare prices.

- **Check for Reviews**: To ensure that your stay meets your expectations, read guest reviews on trusted platforms like **TripAdvisor**, **Hostelworld**, or **Google Reviews**. Reviews provide valuable insight into cleanliness, atmosphere, and the quality of service.

- **Location Matters**: Consider the location of the hostel or guesthouse in relation to your planned activities. If you're in a city like **Bangkok**, you might want to stay near public transport like the

BTS Skytrain or **MRT** subway. In island destinations like **Koh Phi Phi**, proximity to the beach and nightlife is key.

- **Look for Extras**: Many hostels in Thailand offer free Wi-Fi, breakfast, and lockers for your valuables. Some also provide guided tours, cooking classes, or organized activities like pub crawls or beach parties. Look for hostels with added amenities that align with your travel interests.

- **Consider Safety and Security**: While Thailand is generally a safe destination for backpackers, it's important to choose hostels that have security measures in place, such as 24-hour reception, lockers, and secure room access.

Thailand's hostels and guesthouses are perfect for those traveling on a budget or looking for a more social and immersive experience. Whether you're exploring the vibrant cities of Bangkok or Chiang Mai or lounging on the beaches of Koh Samui or Phi Phi, Thailand offers a wide variety of accommodations for every traveler.

5.4 Booking Tips: How to Find the Best Deals

When traveling to Thailand, booking accommodations at the best possible price is essential to making the most of your trip while sticking to your budget. With numerous options available, ranging from luxury resorts to budget hostels, it can be overwhelming to find the right deal. However, with a few strategic tips, you can navigate the booking process and ensure you get the best value for your money. Here are some essential tips on how to find the best deals on accommodations in Thailand.

1. Use Multiple Booking Platforms

Booking accommodations through online travel agencies (OTAs) like **Booking.com**, **Agoda**, **Expedia**, and **Airbnb** can give you a good sense of what's available in your destination. However, prices may vary slightly across platforms due to promotions, different commission structures, and member discounts. To find the best deal, it's a good idea to:

- **Compare prices**: Always check multiple platforms for the same property to ensure you're getting the best price. Some platforms might offer additional perks, like free breakfast, early check-in, or loyalty points, which can add value to your booking.

- **Check hotel websites directly**: Some hotels or resorts offer the best rates when booking directly through their website, cutting out third-party booking fees. Look for price match guarantees, special promotions, or discount codes that may not be listed on OTAs.

- **Sign up for newsletters and deals**: Many booking platforms and hotel chains send special offers and discount codes to subscribers. By subscribing to their newsletters or following them on social media, you can access exclusive promotions.

2. Book Early for Popular Destinations

For popular tourist spots in Thailand, like **Bangkok**, **Phuket**, **Koh Samui**, or **Chiang Mai**, booking early can help secure the best deals, especially during peak tourist seasons (November to February). Prices for accommodations can skyrocket during high season, and popular hotels may sell out quickly.

- **Plan ahead for peak seasons**: If you're traveling during Thailand's peak seasons, book your accommodation several weeks (or even months) in advance to secure lower rates and ensure availability. During **Songkran** (Thai New Year) and **Loy Krathong**, many properties offer discounts for early bookings.

- **Flexible dates**: If your travel dates are flexible, use booking sites that allow you to compare prices across different dates. Avoid booking around public holidays or local festivals when demand is high, and prices may be inflated.

3. Look for Deals on Last-Minute Booking Apps

If you prefer more spontaneity and flexibility with your travel plans, last-minute booking apps and websites can be an excellent way to score great deals. Apps like **HotelTonight**, **Hotwire**, and **Priceline** specialize in offering discounted rates for last-minute bookings.

- **Use last-minute booking apps**: These apps often offer rooms that have been left unsold by hotels at a significant discount. While you may not have as much time to research the property, these apps can offer substantial savings, especially during less busy periods.

- **Last-minute deals for luxury hotels**: If you're looking for luxury stays but don't want to pay full price, last-minute apps often have discounted rates for high-end hotels. You can enjoy a 5-star experience without the hefty price tag, as these hotels will lower their rates closer to check-in to ensure they fill their rooms.

4. Consider Alternative Accommodations

While hotels are the most common form of accommodation in Thailand, considering alternative options like **guesthouses**, **hostels**, and **Airbnb** can help you find more affordable stays that are just as comfortable and enjoyable. These alternatives offer opportunities for cultural immersion and more local experiences.

- **Guesthouses and Homestays**: Guesthouses, especially in places like **Chiang Mai** or **Pai**, are typically more affordable than hotels but still offer excellent service and a more authentic, local experience. Many guesthouses also provide communal areas where you can meet other travelers.

- **Hostels**: If you're traveling solo or as a backpacker, hostels offer an affordable and social way to stay. Popular areas like **Khao San Road** in **Bangkok** and **Phi Phi Islands** have a range of budget-friendly hostels. Many hostels offer free Wi-Fi, complimentary breakfast, and social spaces for guests to interact.

- **Airbnb**: **Airbnb** offers a wide range of accommodations, from entire homes to private rooms in local apartments. By renting an apartment or house, you can save money by cooking your meals and enjoying more space and privacy. Airbnb often offers better rates for longer stays, so it's worth considering if you're spending more than a few days in one location.

- **Eco-resorts**: For travelers seeking a more sustainable experience, **eco-resorts** and **glamping** options are growing in popularity. Many eco-resorts offer an immersive experience in nature without the price tag of luxury resorts. These options can be found in places like **Khao Sok** and **Koh Samui**.

5. Take Advantage of Special Promotions and Discounts

Many booking websites and hotel chains offer ongoing promotions, loyalty rewards, or special discounts for first-time users or repeat guests. These promotions can help you score a great deal on your accommodations.

- **Use loyalty programs**: Sign up for loyalty programs with hotel chains or booking platforms like **Agoda Rewards**, **Booking.com Genius**, or **Hotels.com Rewards**. These programs often offer members exclusive discounts, free upgrades, early check-ins, or late check-outs.

- **Take advantage of credit card deals**: Some credit cards offer travel-related perks, such as discounts on hotel bookings, travel insurance, or points that can be redeemed for free stays. Check if your credit card offers special hotel deals or if there are any partner programs for extra savings.

- **Seek out flash sales**: Websites like **Secret Escapes**, **Groupon**, or **Travelzoo** often feature flash sales that offer significant discounts on hotels and resorts. These deals typically last for a limited time, so it's important to act fast if you want to snag a great deal.

- **Check for off-peak deals**: If you're traveling during the shoulder or off-peak season (such as April, May, or September), many hotels offer reduced rates to attract guests. The off-peak period can be a great time to visit Thailand, as the weather is still pleasant, but you can find more affordable accommodations and avoid crowds.

6. Read Reviews and Look for Hidden Fees

While booking, always read reviews to ensure you're getting the best value for your money. Websites like **TripAdvisor**, **Google Reviews**, and **Yelp** provide useful information from fellow travelers, which can help you avoid unpleasant surprises.

- **Check for hidden fees**: Be mindful of hidden fees such as **resort fees**, **cleaning fees**, or **service charges**, which can sometimes make the final price higher than expected. Always read the fine print before completing your booking, and factor these additional costs into your budget when comparing options.

- **Look for properties with good reviews**: Reviews can help you gauge the overall quality of a property, especially when it comes to things like cleanliness, customer service, and amenities. Booking a well-reviewed property ensures that you're getting the best value for your money.

7. Stay Outside of Popular Tourist Areas

If you're looking to save money and avoid touristy crowds, consider staying a bit further from the main attractions. In cities like **Bangkok** or **Chiang Mai**, staying in neighborhoods slightly outside the city center can save you a significant amount of money. You'll also experience a more authentic side of the city and have the chance to explore lesser-known attractions.

- **Public transportation**: Thailand has an efficient public transportation system, including trains, buses, and the **BTS Skytrain** in **Bangkok**, so staying in less touristy areas still allows easy access to major attractions without the premium price tag of hotels in prime locations.

- **Use local apps and booking sites**: Some local Thai booking platforms, like **Sawadee.com** or **Thai Hotel Link**, might offer better rates on local accommodations compared to global booking sites.

8. Consider Longer Stays for Better Rates

If you're planning to stay in one location for a longer period, many hotels and guesthouses offer discounted rates for extended stays. This is especially common in **Koh Samui**, **Chiang Mai**, and **Krabi**, where long-term visitors can negotiate better deals for stays of 1 week or longer.

- **Negotiate directly**: Don't be afraid to negotiate directly with the hotel or guesthouse if you're staying for a longer period. Many properties offer discounts for long-term stays, especially in more remote areas or off-peak seasons.

- **Look for monthly rates**: Some guesthouses or short-term rental apartments offer **monthly rates**, which can be more affordable than booking daily or weekly. This is particularly useful for digital nomads or those planning an extended stay in places like **Chiang Mai** or **Phuket**.

By following these booking tips, you can find the best deals on accommodations in Thailand and ensure a memorable trip while sticking to your budget. Whether you're using booking platforms, considering alternative accommodation types, or taking advantage of special promotions, Thailand offers a range of accommodation options for every traveler. With a little planning and research, you'll be able to secure the perfect place to stay, leaving you with more funds to explore all that this beautiful country has to offer.

Chapter 6: Cultural Etiquette and Local Customs

6.1 Respecting Thai Culture: Do's and Don'ts

Thailand is a country with a rich cultural heritage, and understanding the local customs and etiquette will help you navigate the country respectfully. Thai culture places great emphasis on manners, politeness, and respect, especially towards elders, religious sites, and the monarchy. Whether you're visiting temples, interacting with locals, or attending social events, it's important to be aware of the cultural norms to ensure a positive experience for both you and the people you encounter.

In this section, we'll highlight the key do's and don'ts that every traveler should keep in mind to show respect for Thailand's culture and customs.

1. The Do's of Thai Culture

1.1. Dress Modestly When Visiting Temples

Thailand is a deeply Buddhist country, and temples are sacred spaces where respectful behavior is expected. Visitors to temples should dress modestly to show respect for the religious practices.

- **What to wear**: For both men and women, it's important to cover shoulders, arms, and legs. Avoid wearing shorts, tank tops, or skirts that are too short. In some temples, such as **Wat Phra Kaew** (The Grand Palace) in **Bangkok**, you may be asked to wear a long-sleeve shirt or cover-up over your clothes if they are not deemed respectful. Many temples will provide or rent out cover-ups for visitors who don't have appropriate clothing.

- **Footwear etiquette**: Always remove your shoes when entering a temple or private home. It's also customary to remove shoes before entering certain businesses, restaurants, or guesthouses, especially in local, traditional areas.

1.2. Wai Gesture (Traditional Greeting)

The **wai** is a traditional Thai greeting in which you place your palms together in a prayer-like gesture and bow your head slightly. It is often used to show respect or to say "hello" and "goodbye."

- **When to use it**: You can offer a **wai** to elders, monks, or people you meet for the first time, especially in formal settings. While it's not required to wai everyone you meet, it's a gesture that shows respect. People will often wai you back, particularly if you're in a formal or respectful setting like a temple or business.

- **How to respond**: If someone offers you a **wai**, it is polite to return the gesture, but if you're unsure or it's an informal setting, a simple **"hello"** with a smile is perfectly acceptable. For foreigners, a **bow** or a slight nod is often a simple and respectful alternative.

1.3. Show Respect to the Royal Family

Thailand has deep reverence for the monarchy, and it's essential to show respect when speaking about or to members of the royal family. Public displays of disrespect towards the monarchy are illegal in Thailand, and the Thai people hold the King and royal family members in high esteem.

- **Do's**: When the Thai national anthem plays, such as during public events or at movie theaters, it's customary to stand up as a sign of respect. Avoid making negative remarks about the King or royal family, as this can be viewed as highly disrespectful.

- **The King's Image**: The King's image is often seen in public places, such as in homes, offices, and government buildings. It's considered disrespectful to point or touch images or portraits of the King, so always approach them with reverence.

1.4. Show Respect to Elders

Respect for elders is deeply ingrained in Thai culture. In both family and social contexts, the elderly are treated with a great deal of reverence.

- **How to treat elders**: Address elders with the honorific **"Khun"**, which is equivalent to "Mr." or "Ms." in English. It's also common for younger people to offer a **wai** to elders as a sign of respect. When speaking to them, show deference and politeness, especially in formal settings.

1.5. Use Polite Language and Behavior

Politeness is highly valued in Thai culture, and using polite language and maintaining a calm, gentle demeanor will help you make a positive impression.

- **Polite words**: The Thai language has gender-specific terms for politeness. For example, men often end sentences with **"krup"**, and women with **"ka"** to show respect. While not essential for basic communication, using these terms can make your conversations more polite and appreciated by locals.

- **Keep a calm demeanor**: Thai people value a calm, composed attitude, so avoid raising your voice or showing anger in public. Keep your tone gentle, and try to maintain a positive and respectful attitude in all situations.

2. The Don'ts of Thai Culture

2.1. Don't Touch the Head

In Thai culture, the head is considered the most sacred part of the body. Touching someone's head, especially a child's, is seen as an invasion of their personal space and a sign of disrespect.

- **What to avoid**: Don't pat someone's head, even if it's done playfully. If you're traveling with children, avoid letting others touch their heads. Always show respect for personal space and refrain from touching anyone's head, including adults.

2.2. Don't Point Your Feet

Feet are considered the lowest and dirtiest part of the body in Thai culture, so it's considered highly disrespectful to point your feet at people or religious objects.

- **What to avoid**: When sitting, don't point your feet towards people, especially elders or monks.

When sitting on the floor, avoid stretching your legs out or crossing your legs in a way that might point your feet at others. Additionally, when visiting a temple, avoid touching religious statues or relics with your feet.

- **What to do**: When greeting someone or showing respect, always sit in a position where your feet are hidden or tucked away. For example, if you're sitting on the floor, it's polite to sit cross-legged or with your feet flat on the floor.

2.3. Don't Raise Your Voice or Publicly Lose Your Temper

Thailand places a strong emphasis on maintaining social harmony and avoiding confrontation. Public displays of anger, aggression, or loud behavior are frowned upon, as they disrupt the calm, respectful environment that Thai society values.

- **What to avoid**: Yelling, arguing, or displaying frustration in public is seen as inappropriate. If you have a problem, try to resolve it privately, calmly, and respectfully. In the case of a dispute, remain composed and polite, even when expressing your dissatisfaction.

2.4. Don't Engage in Public Displays of Affection

While Thai people are generally open and friendly, public displays of affection (PDA) are considered inappropriate in Thai culture, especially in more conservative areas.

- **What to avoid**: Kissing, hugging, or holding hands in public, particularly in religious or formal settings, should be avoided. It's generally acceptable for couples to hold hands in more private settings, but excessive PDA may be seen as disrespectful.

- **What to do**: If you're traveling with a partner, keep physical affection to private spaces. In public, it's best to show affection through polite gestures like holding hands or a gentle touch, but avoid anything more intimate in public.

2.5. Don't Point at People or Objects

Pointing is considered impolite in Thailand. When you point at someone or something, it is seen as disrespectful and can be considered rude.

- **What to avoid**: Avoid pointing with your finger, especially at people or sacred objects like Buddha statues, portraits of the king, or religious artifacts. Instead, if you need to indicate something, use your whole hand, or point with your chin or open hand.

- **What to do**: When pointing or directing someone's attention, gesture with your whole hand or use a subtle nod or chin movement. This shows respect and avoids appearing rude or overly direct.

3. General Cultural Etiquette Tips

- **Respect for monks**: Monks are highly revered in Thailand, and special care should be taken when interacting with them. Women, in particular, should avoid physical contact with monks. When passing by a monk, step aside and allow them to pass first. When visiting a temple, show respect by keeping your voice low and your behavior respectful.

- **Polite bargaining**: In markets and shops, bargaining is a common practice, but it should always be done with a smile and a friendly attitude. Never engage in aggressive or rude negotiations. If the price is too high, politely offer a lower price and maintain a pleasant demeanor.

- **Respect for local traditions and festivals**: When participating in Thai festivals or traditions, it's essential to show respect for the customs involved. Whether you're attending a religious ceremony, participating in Songkran (Thai New Year), or visiting local villages, follow the local etiquette and dress codes to ensure you're acting appropriately.

By understanding and adhering to these **do's and don'ts** of Thai culture, you can demonstrate respect for the local people and traditions, enhancing your experience in the country. Politeness, humility, and a considerate attitude will always be appreciated, and by embracing these cultural norms, you'll be sure to make a positive impression during your travels in Thailand.

6.2 Understanding Thai Religion: Buddhism and Temples

Thailand's culture and daily life are deeply intertwined with religion, and understanding the country's predominant religion—**Theravada Buddhism**—can greatly enhance your experience while traveling in the Kingdom. With around 95% of Thais identifying as Buddhist, religion plays a central role in shaping Thai traditions, behaviors, and attitudes. Temples, or **wats**, are not only religious centers but also cultural landmarks that provide insight into Thailand's spiritual and historical heritage.

In this section, we will explore the significance of Buddhism in Thai culture, the role of temples, and what visitors should know when visiting these sacred sites.

1. Buddhism in Thailand: An Overview

Theravada Buddhism is the oldest and most conservative form of Buddhism, and it is practiced by the majority of Thai people. It focuses on the teachings of the **Buddha** (Siddhartha Gautama), who lived and taught in India around the 5th century BCE. The goal of Buddhism is to achieve enlightenment (Nirvana) by following the **Four Noble Truths** and the **Eightfold Path**—a set of ethical guidelines for living a life free from suffering and desire.

- **The Four Noble Truths**: These teachings form the foundation of Buddhism and address the nature of suffering and its cessation.
    1. **Dukkha (Suffering)**: Life is marked by suffering, whether physical, emotional, or existential.
    2. **Samudaya (Origin of Suffering)**: Suffering is caused by desire, attachment, and ignorance.
    3. **Nirodha (Cessation of Suffering)**: It is possible to end suffering by eliminating desire and attachment.
    4. **Magga (Path to the End of Suffering)**: The way to end suffering is through the Eightfold Path.
- **The Eightfold Path**: This is the practical guide for ethical and mental development that leads to enlightenment. It consists of right understanding,

right intention, right speech, right action, right livelihood, right effort, right mindfulness, and right concentration.

Theravada Buddhism emphasizes monastic life, meditation, and mindfulness. Monks play a crucial role in Thai society as spiritual leaders, teachers, and community figures. Temples, or **wats**, are where monks live, meditate, and carry out their duties, and they are integral to religious and social life.

2. Temples (Wats) in Thailand: Sacred Spaces and Cultural Heritage

Thai temples are not only places of worship but also important centers for education, art, and community activities. The word **"wat"** means temple in Thai, and it generally refers to a complex that includes various buildings such as the **ordination hall** (**ubosot**), the **temple's pagoda** (**chedi**), and the **library**. Temples can be found throughout Thailand, from bustling cities to rural villages, and they serve as spiritual havens for locals and visitors alike.

2.1. Key Elements of a Thai Temple

- **Ubosot (Ordination Hall)**: This is the most important building in a Thai temple. It is where ordination ceremonies take place and where monks gather for communal prayers and meditation. Visitors may not be allowed to enter the **ubosot** unless they are part of the ordained community, but it is often the most beautifully decorated building in the temple complex, adorned with murals depicting the life of the Buddha and various deities.

- **Chedi (Stupa or Pagoda)**: A **chedi** is a tall, often bell-shaped structure that houses relics of the Buddha or important monks. It is a highly symbolic element of Thai temples, representing the Buddha's teachings and his path to enlightenment. Chedis are usually found in temple courtyards and are beautifully decorated, often covered in gold leaf.

- **Viharn (Hall of Images)**: This is the hall where the main Buddha statues or images are housed. The most important Buddha image in the temple is typically seated or reclining in a position that symbolizes his enlightened state. It is common for locals to offer prayers, incense, and flowers before the Buddha statues, a practice known as **wai**.

- **Phra Ubosot (Buddha Hall)**: This is where the monks gather for important ceremonies, such as ordinations or making merit. It is also where the Buddha's teachings are shared. The hall is usually brightly painted and often has intricate woodwork and carvings.

- **Monastic Cells and Meditation Areas**: In addition to the main buildings, most temples include areas where monks live and meditate. These spaces are typically quieter and more secluded, and some may be open to visitors who wish to meditate or learn about Buddhist practices.

- **Sangha (Monastic Community)**: The **sangha** refers to the community of monks and nuns who live in the temple. Monks often serve as spiritual guides for the community, providing teachings on the Buddha's doctrines and offering spiritual advice.

2.2. Common Buddha Statues and Their Meanings

Buddha statues are central to Thai temples, and each posture or gesture has a specific meaning. Visitors to temples may observe various statues of the Buddha in different postures:

- **Seated Buddha (Meditation Posture)**: The Buddha is shown seated in a cross-legged position with hands resting in his lap, representing meditation and enlightenment.

- **Standing Buddha**: A Buddha in the standing position signifies the Buddha's compassion for humanity and his readiness to teach others. It is also a representation of his victory over temptation and the ultimate realization of the truth.

- **Reclining Buddha**: This represents the Buddha's last moments before achieving Nirvana. The reclining position is symbolic of rest after the hard work of meditation and the final moment of enlightenment.

- **Laughing Buddha**: Often seen in public places or home altars, the laughing Buddha is not a representation of the historical Buddha but rather a symbol of happiness, prosperity, and contentment.

3. Visiting Temples in Thailand: Etiquette and Respect

When visiting a temple in Thailand, it's important to follow the local customs and behave respectfully. Below are some guidelines to help you navigate the experience appropriately:

3.1. Dress Modestly

As mentioned earlier, modest dress is required when entering a temple. Cover your shoulders, arms, and knees. Women should avoid wearing sleeveless tops, shorts, or skirts above the knee, while men should wear long pants or shorts that cover the knee. Some temples may provide cover-ups or ask visitors to wear appropriate attire if they arrive in unsuitable clothing.

3.2. Remove Your Shoes

Before entering any building within a temple complex, it's customary to remove your shoes. This is a sign of respect, as it helps to keep the temple clean and signifies that you are entering a sacred space.

3.3. Don't Touch the Buddha Images

It's considered highly disrespectful to touch Buddha statues, especially in temples. Only monks and ordained individuals are permitted to touch the Buddha. As a visitor, simply showing respect through a **wai** gesture or by bowing is sufficient.

3.4. Show Respect to Monks

Monks hold a high place of honor in Thai society, and showing respect towards them is a fundamental aspect of Buddhist etiquette. If you see a monk, it's polite to offer a slight bow or **wai**. Avoid direct physical contact with monks, especially women. Buddhist teachings prohibit physical contact between monks and women, so women should never hand something directly to a monk;

instead, they should place it on a table or offer it indirectly.

3.5. Maintain a Calm and Quiet Demeanor

Temples are places for meditation and reflection, so it's important to maintain a quiet, calm demeanor. Speaking loudly, laughing, or engaging in disruptive behavior is considered disrespectful.

3.6. Make Offerings and Donations

Many visitors to temples make offerings to the Buddha, such as flowers, incense, or candles, as part of a practice called **making merit**. This act is believed to generate good karma and spiritual merit. While donations are encouraged to support the temple, they are voluntary. If you wish to make a donation, place the money in the donation box or hand it to the monk in a respectful manner.

4. The Role of Monks in Thai Society

Monks in Thailand are central to the practice of Buddhism, and they play a significant role in the spiritual life of the country. Many Thai men will spend some time as monks, whether for a short period or a more extended commitment, as part of their religious duties. The process of ordination is seen as an important rite of passage, and during their time as monks, they follow strict rules of behavior, including celibacy, meditation, and almsgiving.

- **Almsgiving**: One of the most visible roles of monks in Thai culture is their daily practice of almsgiving, where they walk through local neighborhoods and receive food offerings from the community. Thai people will often offer food, such as rice, fruit, or snacks, as a way to make merit.

- **Monastic Teachings**: Monks also provide teachings to the lay community. In many temples, monks lead meditation sessions, teach Buddhist principles, and provide spiritual counseling to those seeking guidance.

5. Buddhist Holidays and Festivals in Thailand

Buddhism is celebrated through various holidays and festivals that honor the Buddha and Buddhist teachings. Some important holidays include:

- **Makha Bucha**: This festival celebrates the Buddha's first sermon to 1,250 of his disciples. It's marked by prayer, meditation, and offering ceremonies.

- **Visakha Bucha**: This is one of the most significant Buddhist holidays, commemorating the birth, enlightenment, and death of the Buddha. It's observed with temple visits, candle-lit processions, and teachings.

- **Asalha Puja**: This marks the Buddha's first sermon and the beginning of the Buddhist monastic community. It's an important day for meditation and making merit.

Understanding Thai Buddhism and the cultural importance of temples can make your visit to Thailand more meaningful. By respecting the sacred practices and etiquette associated with Buddhism, you will not only have a deeper connection to the culture but will also demonstrate respect to the Thai people and their religious traditions. Whether you're visiting a temple in **Bangkok**, trekking to a remote mountain monastery in **Chiang Mai**, or exploring ancient ruins in **Ayutthaya**, the experience of Buddhism in Thailand is a beautiful way to enrich your travels.

6.3 Dress Code: What to Wear in Different Settings

Thailand's culture places great emphasis on modesty, respect, and appropriate attire, and understanding the dress code for various settings can help you navigate social situations, religious sites, and the tropical climate with ease. While the country is known for its warm hospitality and laid-back atmosphere, dressing appropriately is a sign of respect for the local customs, and it can also enhance your experience as you explore different parts of the country.

In this section, we'll explore what to wear in various settings, including temples, beaches, cities, rural areas, and special events, so you can always feel confident and respectful of Thai traditions and climate.

1. Dress Code for Visiting Temples and Religious Sites

Temples, or **wats**, are sacred spaces in Thailand, and it's important to dress modestly when visiting these religious sites. Whether you're exploring the magnificent **Wat Phra Kaew** (Temple of the Emerald Buddha) in **Bangkok** or the tranquil **Wat Doi Suthep** in **Chiang Mai**, adhering to the dress code will ensure that you show respect for the culture and religion.

1.1. General Guidelines for Temples:

- **Cover your shoulders and knees**: Both men and women should wear clothing that covers their shoulders and knees. Sleeveless tops, shorts, skirts, and dresses that are too short are generally considered disrespectful. Opt for T-shirts or long-sleeve shirts and long pants or knee-length skirts.

- **Avoid tight or revealing clothing**: Avoid wearing clothing that is too tight, short, or revealing. Thailand's culture emphasizes modesty, especially in religious settings, so aim for clothing that is comfortable but respectful.
- **No hats or sunglasses**: When entering a temple, remove your hat and sunglasses as a sign of respect. You may also be asked to take off your shoes before entering certain temple buildings.
- **Footwear**: Always remove your shoes before entering a temple building. In many temples, you'll see designated areas where visitors can leave their shoes.
- **What to Wear for Women**: Women should avoid wearing dresses or tops with low necklines or sleeveless styles. A long skirt or a pair of long pants paired with a modest blouse is appropriate. If you forget to bring modest attire, many temples provide cover-ups or shawls for visitors to borrow.
- **What to Wear for Men**: Men should avoid wearing shorts or sleeveless shirts. Long pants and a short- or long-sleeve shirt are more appropriate. For a more formal temple visit, a collared shirt and dress pants can be a good choice.

1.2. Specific Examples of What to Wear

- **Wat Phra Kaew, Bangkok**: At this iconic temple, visitors are expected to wear long pants and long sleeves. A T-shirt or shirt with sleeves is acceptable, but make sure to avoid anything too casual (like flip-flops or tank tops).
- **Wat Doi Suthep, Chiang Mai**: A simple outfit such as a long-sleeve shirt and long pants or a long skirt is ideal. Since the weather can be cooler in the mountains, consider bringing a light jacket as well.

2. Dress Code for Beach and Island Visits

Thailand is famous for its beautiful beaches and islands, such as **Phuket**, **Koh Samui**, **Koh Phi Phi**, and **Koh Tao**. While casual beachwear is perfect for lounging by the water, it's important to keep in mind the cultural expectations when you're away from the beach or near religious sites.

2.1. Beachwear Guidelines:

- **Swimwear**: On the beach or by the pool, swimsuits (bikinis, trunks, etc.) are perfectly fine. However, avoid wearing swimwear away from the beach or pool areas, especially when walking through restaurants, shops, or temples.
- **Cover-Up for Women and Men**: If you're leaving the beach or pool area, it's respectful to cover up. Women can wear a beach cover-up, sarong, or sundress, while men should wear

shorts and a T-shirt. This is important when entering restaurants, shops, or walking around town.
- **Footwear**: On the beach, flip-flops or sandals are common, but when entering restaurants or temples, you should wear appropriate footwear. Closed-toe shoes or sandals are recommended for dining out or for visits to cultural sites.

2.2. Example of Beachwear Etiquette

- **Koh Phi Phi**: While it's perfectly acceptable to wear a bikini or swim trunks on the beach or in the pool, remember to cover up with a sarong or T-shirt when walking around the island, especially if you're heading into shops, cafés, or temples.
- **Koh Samui**: The dress code for beach clubs and restaurants in Koh Samui can vary, but generally, it's okay to wear a swimsuit and a cover-up while walking around the beach. However, more upscale restaurants may require guests to wear smart casual attire.

3. Dress Code for Urban Areas (Bangkok, Chiang Mai, etc.)

When you're in urban centers like **Bangkok, Chiang Mai**, or **Phuket Town**, the dress code is a bit more relaxed, but it's still important to dress appropriately for both cultural sites and social situations.

3.1. General City Etiquette:

- **Smart Casual**: In restaurants, bars, and malls, smart casual attire is generally appropriate. For men, this can include collared shirts and trousers, and for women, a nice blouse and jeans or a skirt. Many restaurants and upscale shopping centers may not allow flip-flops or overly casual attire.
- **Respectful and Modest**: While in the city, it's important to dress modestly, particularly in places where you're interacting with the local community, such as temples, markets, or cultural centers. Avoid excessively revealing or offensive clothing.
- **Layer Up in Air-Conditioned Spaces**: In places with air-conditioning (such as shopping malls, cinemas, or hotels), you may find that the temperatures are quite cold inside, even when it's hot outside. It's a good idea to bring along a light sweater, scarf, or jacket when venturing into these spaces.

3.2. Example of Urban Attire

- **Bangkok**: Bangkok is a bustling metropolis with a wide variety of settings, from upscale restaurants and shopping malls to street food stalls. In upscale malls like **Siam Paragon** or **CentralWorld**, it's best to wear a smart casual outfit. A collared shirt and trousers for men or a

nice blouse and skirt or pants for women will suffice. When visiting temples like **Wat Arun** or **Wat Phra Kaew**, remember to adhere to the modest dress code (long pants/skirts, covered shoulders).
- **Chiang Mai**: Chiang Mai offers a more relaxed atmosphere compared to Bangkok, but it's still advisable to dress neatly. In the Old City or during cultural events, it's common to see visitors in casual yet respectful outfits like light dresses, T-shirts, and long pants or skirts.

4. Dress Code for Rural Areas and Villages

When visiting rural areas, hill tribe villages, or more remote parts of Thailand, it's important to dress respectfully for both cultural reasons and practical concerns. In some villages, modesty is highly valued, and visitors should aim to blend in with the local customs.

4.1. Modesty and Respect for Local Traditions

- **Cover Your Shoulders and Knees**: In rural areas, dress modestly, especially when visiting temples or local homes. Women should wear longer skirts or pants and avoid revealing tops, while men should avoid wearing shorts or tank tops.
- **Practical Clothing**: Rural areas may involve outdoor activities like hiking or exploring national

parks, so consider wearing comfortable, breathable clothing and sturdy shoes. If you plan to visit a hill tribe village, it's also a good idea to wear closed-toe shoes and lightweight clothing that will keep you cool in the tropical climate.

4.2. Example of Rural Attire

- **Hill Tribe Villages in Northern Thailand**: If you're visiting a hill tribe village in **Chiang Mai** or **Chiang Rai**, it's respectful to wear long pants, closed shoes, and a modest top. These villages tend to be more conservative, so dressing appropriately is essential to show respect for local customs.
- **Khao Sok National Park**: For exploring the jungle or trekking through **Khao Sok National Park**, wear lightweight, breathable clothing, along with sturdy shoes for hiking. Since the weather can be humid and rainy, it's also a good idea to bring a light rain jacket or poncho.

5. Dress Code for Special Events and Festivals

Thailand's festivals, from **Songkran** (Thai New Year) to **Loy Krathong** (Lantern Festival), are significant cultural events that often involve both local participants and tourists. When attending a festival or special cultural event, consider the following dress codes:

- **Songkran Festival**: During Songkran, you'll likely get wet, as water fights are a central part of the celebration. Dress in comfortable, light clothing that you don't mind getting soaked. Many people wear casual clothes like T-shirts and shorts, but be mindful of the public setting and the need to remain respectful, even in the middle of the festivities.

- **Loy Krathong Festival**: For this festival, you'll often see people dressed in traditional Thai clothing, especially in **Sukhothai** and **Chiang Mai**. Wearing something formal, like a nice dress or collared shirt and pants, can be a great way to blend in with locals, especially if you plan to participate in the evening processions.

Thailand's dress codes are influenced by both the tropical climate and the country's deep-rooted Buddhist traditions. Whether you're visiting temples, relaxing on a beach, or exploring bustling cities, dressing appropriately shows respect for the culture and enhances your travel experience. Keep in mind that modest, comfortable attire is the key to navigating the different settings and environments that Thailand offers, from sacred religious sites to vibrant social scenes.

6.4 Language: Basic Thai Phrases for Travelers

Although many people in Thailand's major tourist destinations speak English, knowing a few basic phrases in Thai can go a long way in enhancing your experience and showing respect for the local culture. Thai is a tonal language, meaning that the meaning of a word can change depending on the tone used. While this may seem challenging, don't be discouraged—simple phrases with the correct pronunciation can still help you get by and form positive connections with locals.

In this section, we'll cover some of the most useful and commonly used Thai phrases for travelers. These phrases will help you navigate daily interactions, whether you're ordering food, asking for directions, or making polite small talk.

1. Basic Greetings and Courtesies

In Thai culture, polite greetings and showing respect are essential. The **wai** gesture, where the palms are pressed together in a prayer-like position, is commonly used, but not required for every greeting. However, it is important to be mindful of how you greet others in various contexts.

1.1. Hello and Goodbye

- **Sawasdee (สวัสดี)** [sa-wat-dee] – **Hello**
    - You can use **sawasdee** for both **hello** and **goodbye**. When speaking to a

woman, it's polite to add **"ka"** at the end (sawasdee ka), and when speaking to a man, use **"krub"** (sawasdee krub).
- Example: **Sawasdee ka** (Hello, woman) or **Sawasdee krub** (Hello, man).

1.2. Thank You

- **Khob khun (ขอบคุณ)** [khob-khun] – **Thank you**
  - Add **"ka"** for women or **"krub"** for men at the end of the phrase for added politeness.
  - Example: **Khob khun ka** (Thank you, woman) or **Khob khun krub** (Thank you, man).

1.3. How Are You?

- **Sawasdee, sabai dee mai? (สวัสดี สบายดี ไหม?)** [sa-wat-dee, sa-bai dee mai?] – **Hello, how are you?**
  - "Sabai dee" means **good** or **comfortable**, and **mai** is a question word.
  - Response: **Sabai dee (สบายดี)** [sa-bai dee] – **I'm fine.**

1.4. Goodbye

- **La korn (ลาก่อน)** [laa-gon] – **Goodbye**

- o This phrase is more formal and used less frequently than **sawasdee** to say goodbye.

2. Polite Expressions

Thai people are known for their politeness, and adding **"krub"** (for men) or **"ka"** (for women) to phrases makes them more polite and respectful. These particles are often used in the Thai language to indicate respect in social situations.

2.1. Excuse Me / Sorry

- **Khau-thot (ขอโทษ)** [kaw-thot] – **Excuse me / Sorry**
    - o This phrase can be used to apologize or get someone's attention.
    - o Example: **Khau-thot, chan chao mae khong chan** (Excuse me, I need something).

2.2. Yes

- **Chai (ใช่)** [chai] – **Yes**

2.3. No

- **Mai chai (ไม่ใช่)** [mai chai] – **No**

2.4. Please

- **Chao (ช่วย)** [chuay] – **Please**
    - Often used when asking for help or when making a request.
    - Example: **Chao chuay pom duai** (Please help me).

3. Ordering Food and Drinks

Food is a central part of Thai culture, and knowing a few phrases to help you order at restaurants or street stalls will make your experience much smoother.

3.1. I Would Like

- **Ao (เอา)** [ao] – **I want / I would like**
    - Example: **Ao gai** (I want chicken).

3.2. How Much is This?

- **Nee tao rai? (นี่เท่าไหร่?)** [nee tao rai?] – **How much is this?**

3.3. Delicious

- **Aroy (อร่อย)** [a-roy] – **Delicious**
    - When you find food you enjoy, you can tell the vendor, **Aroy mak** (very delicious).

3.4. Water

- **Nam (น้ำ)** [nam] – **Water**

- Example: **Nam suai** (clean water) or **Nam preaw** (sweet water).

3.5. Food

- **Ah-han (อาหาร)** [a-han] – **Food**

4. Directions and Transportation

If you're exploring Thailand, knowing how to ask for directions or navigate the transportation system will be incredibly helpful.

4.1. Where is…?

- **…Yoo tee nai? (…อยู่ที่ไหน?)** [yoo tee nai?] – **Where is…?**
  - Example: **Wai nai yoo tee nai?** (Where is the bathroom?).

4.2. How Do I Get to…?

- **Pai…yang ngai? (ไป…ยังไง?)** [pai … yang ngai?] – **How do I get to…?**
  - Example: **Pai Chiang Mai yang ngai?** (How do I get to Chiang Mai?).

4.3. Taxi

- **Taxi (แท็กซี่)** [taxi] – **Taxi**

- You can simply say "taxi" when trying to hail a taxi, but it's helpful to know how to negotiate prices or ask for the meter.
- Example: **Khob khun krub, chai meter mai?** (Thank you, do you use the meter?).

4.4. Bus

- **Rot meuk (รถเมล์)** [rot meh] – **Bus**

5. Numbers and Currency

Learning the numbers will help you with bargaining at markets, shopping, and paying for services.

5.1. Numbers 1-10

- 1 – **Nung (หนึ่ง)** [nung]
- 2 – **Sung (สอง)** [song]
- 3 – **Sam (สาม)** [saam]
- 4 – **Si (สี่)** [see]
- 5 – **Ha (ห้า)** [haa]
- 6 – **Hok (หก)** [hok]
- 7 – **Jet (เจ็ด)** [jet]
- 8 – **Bpaet (แปด)** [paet]
- 9 – **Kao (เก้า)** [kao]
- 10 – **Sip (สิบ)** [sip]

5.2. Prices

- Price – **Ra-kha (ราคา)** [ra-kha]

- **How much?** – **Tao-rai? (เท่าไหร่?)** [tao-rai?]
- **Cheap** – **Tao (ถูก)** [took]
- **Expensive** – **Pang (แพง)** [paeng]

6. Emergency Phrases

In case of emergencies, knowing how to ask for help can be vital for your safety and well-being.

6.1. Help!

- **Choo-ay! (ช่วย!)** [chua-y!] – **Help!**

6.2. I'm Lost

- **Chan long thaang (ฉันหลงทาง)** [chan long taang] – **I'm lost.**

6.3. I Need a Doctor

- **Chan tong gaan mo (ฉันต้องการหมอ)** [chan tong gaan maw] – **I need a doctor.**

6.4. Where is the Police?

- **Ror chao yoo tee nai? (โรงพักอยู่ที่ไหน?)** [rong-pak yoo tee nai?] – **Where is the police station?**

While many people in Thailand, particularly in tourist areas, can communicate in English, making an effort to speak a few words of Thai will go a long way in showing respect for the local culture and people. Whether you're ordering food, asking for directions, or simply greeting someone, using these basic phrases will enhance your travel experience and create a deeper connection with the people you meet. So, don't be shy—try out some of these phrases and enjoy the warmth and friendliness of Thailand!

Chapter 7: Shopping, Nightlife, and Entertainment

7.1 Markets and Shopping: From Street Stalls to Malls

Shopping in Thailand is an experience unlike any other, where you can find everything from handcrafted souvenirs and local street food to luxury brands and cutting-edge fashion. Whether you're looking for a unique keepsake, something trendy, or simply want to explore Thailand's vibrant retail scene, there is something for every type of shopper. Thailand's shopping landscape ranges from bustling markets and street stalls to high-end malls, and each offers a distinctive experience.

In this section, we'll explore the different types of shopping experiences you can have in Thailand, from open-air markets to modern shopping centers, providing you with a complete guide to shopping in this fascinating country.

1. Street Markets: The Heart of Thai Shopping Culture

Thailand is famous for its street markets, which are not only great for shopping but also offer a cultural immersion that can't be found in more commercialized shopping areas. These markets are where locals shop, where you'll find authentic souvenirs, fresh produce, unique textiles, handmade goods, and street food. Here are some of the best and most iconic street markets you should visit during your trip.

1.1. Chatuchak Weekend Market (Bangkok)

One of the largest markets in the world, **Chatuchak Weekend Market** (often called **JJ Market**) is a must-visit for anyone in Bangkok. It is an eclectic market that features over 8,000 stalls selling everything imaginable—clothes, accessories, furniture, antiques, plants, pets, and so much more. It's an excellent place to shop for affordable souvenirs, artisan goods, and locally made products.

- **What to Buy**: You can find a variety of items here, including vintage clothing, handmade jewelry, Thai silk, handcrafted home décor, and local handicrafts. For those with a sweet tooth, there are street food stalls offering Thai desserts like **mango sticky rice**, **coconut ice cream**, and **crispy roti**.

- **Tips for Visiting**: Be prepared to spend a few hours wandering through the maze of lanes. Wear comfortable shoes, as the market can get crowded and hot. It's also wise to bargain at this market—haggling is expected, and you can often get discounts if you're persistent.

1.2. Night Markets

Night markets are a staple of Thai shopping culture, especially in cities like Bangkok, Chiang Mai, and Pattaya. These markets come alive in the evening, offering a wide variety of products and food items. They provide a more relaxed shopping experience compared to the daytime hustle of busy malls and markets.

- **Asiatique the Riverfront (Bangkok)**: Located along the Chao Phraya River, **Asiatique** is an upscale night market that combines the charm of a traditional Thai market with modern shopping and dining. It offers everything from fashion, jewelry, and handicrafts to home décor and artwork.

    - **What to Buy**: You'll find a variety of clothing, accessories, artwork, and home furnishings. Asiatique is also home to many food stalls, where you can enjoy authentic Thai dishes, seafood, and desserts. It's also a great place to buy souvenirs and handcrafted items.

    - **Tips for Visiting**: The market can get busy in the evening, especially on weekends, so plan your visit accordingly.

The riverfront setting also provides great photo opportunities, so don't forget your camera.

- **Sunday Walking Street Market (Chiang Mai)**: Chiang Mai's **Sunday Walking Street Market** is an iconic destination for both locals and tourists. Located in the heart of the Old City, this market opens every Sunday evening and stretches along Ratchadamnoen Road, featuring hundreds of stalls selling everything from clothes to traditional crafts.

    - **What to Buy**: Handmade products such as **silver jewelry**, **Thai wooden crafts**, **ceramics**, and **scarves** are abundant. The market is also a great place to sample local street food, including **Khao Soi** (Chiang Mai's famous noodle soup) and **sticky rice dumplings**.

    - **Tips for Visiting**: The Sunday market is a great way to explore the city's artsy side. Bring cash, as most vendors do not accept credit cards, and take your time to explore the wide array of handcrafted goods.

1.3. Floating Markets

Floating markets offer a unique and picturesque shopping experience. These markets take place on boats floating along canals or rivers, where vendors sell everything from fruits and vegetables to souvenirs and Thai snacks.

- **Damnoen Saduak Floating Market (Ratchaburi)**: The most famous floating market in Thailand, **Damnoen Saduak** is located about 100 kilometers southwest of Bangkok. Here, vendors sell products from their boats, offering everything from fresh produce and flowers to handmade goods.

    - **What to Buy**: Local fruits like **mangoes**, **pineapples**, and **coconut sweets** are a popular purchase. You'll also find unique Thai souvenirs such as **wooden carvings** and **Thai silk scarves**.

    - **Tips for Visiting**: Arrive early to avoid the crowds, as the market gets quite busy later in the morning. A boat ride through the market is the best way to experience it, so consider booking a boat tour.

- **Amphawa Floating Market (Samut Songkhram)**: This market, about 90 minutes from Bangkok, offers a more laid-back atmosphere than Damnoen Saduak. It's popular among locals, and here you'll find traditional Thai food, as well as handmade crafts and clothing.

- **What to Buy**: Apart from fresh produce, **Amphawa** is known for its **Thai desserts** like **roti sai mai** (Thai cotton candy), and grilled seafood.

- **Tips for Visiting**: The market is best visited in the late afternoon or evening, when the vendors light their boats with colorful lanterns. This creates a magical atmosphere perfect for photos.

2. Modern Shopping Malls: Luxury and Global Brands

While street markets offer a more authentic Thai shopping experience, **shopping malls** in Thailand cater to those looking for luxury, designer brands, and international retailers. Many of the country's malls are modern and massive, housing international brands, high-end fashion, electronics, and entertainment options.

2.1. Siam Paragon (Bangkok)

Siam Paragon is one of the largest and most luxurious shopping malls in Bangkok, located in the heart of the city near **Siam Square**. This iconic mall is a must-visit for anyone interested in shopping for high-end brands, fashion, and entertainment.

- **What to Buy**: You'll find everything from luxury fashion brands like **Gucci**, **Louis Vuitton**, and **Chanel** to high-tech gadgets, gourmet food, and unique Thai designer items. Siam Paragon also features an extensive selection of Thai and international restaurants, as well as a **seafood market** and a **cinema**.

- **Tips for Visiting**: The mall can get crowded, especially on weekends. Take your time to explore the various sections of the mall, from the luxury boutiques to the lower floors dedicated to affordable fashion and souvenirs.

2.2. CentralWorld (Bangkok)

CentralWorld is another major shopping center in **Bangkok**, located near **Siam Square**. As one of the largest malls in Southeast Asia, it is home to a wide variety of stores, ranging from budget-friendly brands to high-end fashion labels.

- **What to Buy**: You'll find everything from trendy clothing, gadgets, and home décor to beauty products. The mall also has a number of restaurants offering both local and international cuisines.

- **Tips for Visiting**: CentralWorld is often less crowded than Siam Paragon, making it a great choice for those looking to shop in a more relaxed atmosphere. The mall also hosts seasonal promotions and events, so check their schedule to catch any special deals.

2.3. ICONSIAM (Bangkok)

ICONSIAM is one of Bangkok's newest luxury malls, located along the **Chao Phraya River**. This sophisticated mall combines high-end shopping with a cultural experience, offering both international luxury brands and local Thai designers.

- **What to Buy**: In addition to luxury fashion and lifestyle brands, ICONSIAM has a section dedicated to **local Thai artisans** and designers, making it a great place to pick up unique, high-quality souvenirs. The mall also has a large **supermarket** offering gourmet food from around the world.

- **Tips for Visiting**: ICONSIAM is a great place to shop if you're looking for a combination of global and local goods. Don't miss the **Siam Takashimaya** department store, which has exclusive offerings not found in other malls.

3. Bargaining: Haggling in Thailand's Markets

Bargaining is a common practice in Thailand's markets, especially for items like clothes, souvenirs, and accessories. While bargaining is not typically done in high-end malls or supermarkets, you will find that street vendors, night markets, and floating markets are more open to negotiation.

3.1. How to Bargain

- **Start Low**: When you start haggling, aim for about half the price of the vendor's first offer. This gives you room to negotiate up to a fair price.
- **Be Polite and Smile**: Bargaining is a friendly, polite process in Thailand. Always remain calm, smile, and show respect to the vendor, as a pleasant attitude can lead to a better deal.
- **Don't Show Too Much Interest**: If you really like an item, try not to show too much excitement or eagerness to buy it, as this could make the vendor less likely to offer a discount.
- **Cash is King**: Cash payments are often preferred in markets, and some vendors may offer small discounts if you pay in cash.

Thailand offers a diverse shopping experience that caters to all budgets and tastes. Whether you prefer the hustle and bustle of street markets, the convenience of modern shopping malls, or the charm of floating markets, you'll find plenty of opportunities to shop for everything from souvenirs to luxury goods. Embrace the shopping culture, practice polite bargaining, and enjoy the thrill of discovering unique items across this beautiful country.

7.2 Nightlife: Bars, Clubs, and Shows in Thailand

Thailand's nightlife is legendary, offering a wide range of options for all kinds of revelers—from relaxed beach bars and cultural shows to high-energy nightclubs and sophisticated rooftop lounges. Whether you're looking to dance the night away, enjoy a quiet drink, or experience traditional Thai performances, the country's vibrant nightlife scene will cater to every taste. With popular hotspots in cities like **Bangkok**, **Pattaya**, **Phuket**, and **Chiang Mai**, Thailand is a destination that comes alive after dark.

In this section, we will explore the best nightlife experiences Thailand has to offer, including bars, nightclubs, and traditional performances that will make your nights in the Kingdom unforgettable.

1. Bars and Pubs: Relaxed and Lively Spots for Socializing

Thailand is known for its wide variety of bars and pubs, each offering its own unique vibe. Whether you prefer a laid-back beach bar or a high-energy spot with live music, you'll find plenty of options to unwind and enjoy a drink. Here's a look at some of the most popular types of bars in Thailand.

1.1. Rooftop Bars: Breathtaking Views and Chic Atmospheres

Rooftop bars are the perfect way to enjoy a cocktail while soaking in panoramic views of Thailand's skyline or coastal scenery. These upscale venues often feature stylish décor, a great atmosphere, and live music or DJs.

- **Sky Bar at Lebua State Tower (Bangkok)**: One of the most iconic rooftop bars in Thailand, **Sky Bar** at the **Lebua State Tower** offers incredible views of the Chao Phraya River and the Bangkok skyline. It's the perfect place for a sunset cocktail, but be prepared for slightly higher prices due to its premium location. This bar also gained fame for its appearance in the movie *The Hangover Part II*.

    - **Vibe**: Sophisticated, glamorous, and perfect for special occasions.

- - **What to Expect**: Signature cocktails, a panoramic view, and a lively ambiance.
- **Octave Rooftop Lounge & Bar (Phuket)**: Located on the rooftop of the **Marriott Hotel** in **Phuket**, this bar offers stunning views of **Karon Beach** and the surrounding areas. With a trendy vibe and excellent cocktails, it's a popular spot for both tourists and locals.
  - **Vibe**: Casual yet chic, with stunning views of the beach.
  - **What to Expect**: Delicious cocktails, relaxed seating, and DJs.
- **Sirocco (Bangkok)**: Located on the 63rd floor of the **Lebua State Tower**, **Sirocco** is one of the highest rooftop restaurants and bars in Thailand. It offers an elegant dining experience paired with a sophisticated bar setting.
  - **Vibe**: Upscale and refined.
  - **What to Expect**: A lavish dining experience with impeccable cocktails.

1.2. Beach Bars and Island Bars: Relaxed Vibes by the Sea

Thailand's beaches are home to some of the most relaxed and fun beach bars, especially in islands like **Koh Samui**, **Phuket**, and **Koh Phi Phi**. These spots offer the perfect mix of stunning views, great drinks, and live music. Whether you're looking for a laid-back place to watch the sunset or a lively bar to socialize, Thailand's beach bars deliver.

- **Rock Bar (Phuket)**: Located along the stunning **Kamala Beach**, **Rock Bar** offers great drinks, a chilled-out vibe, and a fantastic view of the ocean. This bar is famous for its relaxed atmosphere and is a great spot to enjoy a sunset cocktail.
    - **Vibe**: Laid-back and cozy, ideal for unwinding by the beach.
    - **What to Expect**: Chilled-out music, casual dress, and oceanfront views.
- **Reggae Bar (Koh Samui)**: Situated in **Chaweng Beach**, **Reggae Bar** is a popular hangout for those who enjoy a casual, fun atmosphere with live reggae music, cheap drinks, and plenty of good vibes.
    - **Vibe**: Fun, casual, and very friendly.
    - **What to Expect**: Live reggae music, dancing, and a laid-back crowd.
- **The Beach Bar (Koh Phi Phi)**: This bar offers a perfect setting for enjoying a beachside drink while watching the sunset. Located just steps from the water on **Phi Phi Don**, the bar is known for its fun atmosphere, cheap drinks, and vibrant crowd.

- **Vibe**: Relaxed, friendly, and ideal for meeting fellow travelers.
- **What to Expect**: Beachfront location, casual vibe, and music.

1.3. Craft Beer and Pub Bars

For beer lovers, Thailand's craft beer scene has been growing, with an increasing number of bars and pubs offering local and international craft beers. In cities like **Bangkok** and **Chiang Mai**, there are plenty of spots to enjoy a cold one, catch live music, or hang out with friends.

- **Mikkeller Bangkok (Bangkok)**: A haven for craft beer lovers, **Mikkeller** offers a rotating selection of international and local craft beers, including many unique brews that can't be found elsewhere in the city.
    - **Vibe**: Cozy, intimate, and great for craft beer enthusiasts.
    - **What to Expect**: A wide selection of craft beers and an inviting atmosphere.
- **The Beer Vault (Pattaya)**: Located in **Pattaya**, this pub features an impressive selection of craft beers from both local breweries and international labels, along with an extensive menu of comfort food.
    - **Vibe**: Casual and fun.

- **What to Expect**: Great beer selection, sports on TV, and a friendly crowd.

2. Nightclubs: Dance the Night Away

Thailand's nightclub scene is famous for its energy and diverse range of music, attracting partygoers from all over the world. From high-energy EDM clubs to more laid-back spots with live music, you'll find a club that fits your style, whether you're looking to dance until dawn or simply enjoy a cocktail in a lively environment.

2.1. EDM and Dance Clubs

For those who love electronic dance music, Thailand has some of the best clubs in Asia, featuring world-class DJs, cutting-edge sound systems, and an exciting party atmosphere. Whether you're in Bangkok, **Phuket**, or **Koh Samui**, you'll find plenty of options to dance all night.

- **Onyx (Bangkok)**: Located in the bustling **RCA (Royal City Avenue)** entertainment district, **Onyx** is one of Bangkok's most famous nightclubs, known for its incredible light shows, EDM music, and international DJs.
    - **Vibe**: High-energy, with an international crowd.

- **What to Expect**: EDM music, top-notch sound systems, and a clubbing experience you won't forget.
- **Illuzion (Phuket)**: As one of the biggest nightclubs in **Phuket**, **Illuzion** is famous for its massive dance floor, international DJ sets, and amazing visual effects. It's the place to be if you want to experience an unforgettable night out.
  - **Vibe**: High-energy, top-tier clubbing experience.
  - **What to Expect**: Big-name DJs, great vibes, and a packed dance floor.

2.2. Live Music Venues

If you prefer a more relaxed but still lively experience, Thailand also boasts plenty of live music venues where you can enjoy everything from jazz and blues to rock and Thai folk music.

- **Saxophone Pub (Bangkok)**: Located near the **Victory Monument, Saxophone Pub** is one of the oldest and most beloved live music venues in Bangkok. Known for its top-notch jazz and blues performances, this venue attracts both locals and tourists.
  - **Vibe**: Relaxed, intimate, and cozy with a great live music experience.

- - **What to Expect**: Live jazz, blues, and cocktails.
- **The Chiang Mai Jazz Festival (Chiang Mai)**: If you're in Chiang Mai, the **Chiang Mai Jazz Festival** is a must-visit. This event features a wide range of jazz musicians and performances in a festive setting. Outside the festival, **The North Gate Jazz Co-Op** is a favorite spot for live jazz music.
  - **Vibe**: Casual, lively, with great music.
  - **What to Expect**: Live jazz performances, an intimate crowd, and a welcoming atmosphere.

3. Shows and Cultural Performances

For those looking for an entertainment experience that showcases Thai culture, Thailand offers an array of traditional performances, cabaret shows, and cultural spectacles. These events are a fun way to learn about the country's rich cultural heritage and enjoy a night of entertainment.

3.1. Traditional Thai Shows

- **Siam Niramit (Bangkok)**: One of the most impressive cultural shows in Thailand, **Siam Niramit** offers a spectacular performance that tells the story of Thailand's history, culture, and spirituality. The show features traditional dance, music, and stunning special effects.

- **Vibe**: Cultural, family-friendly, and highly entertaining.
- **What to Expect**: Traditional performances, elaborate costumes, and incredible stage production.
- **Khon (Traditional Thai Masked Dance)**: If you're in **Bangkok**, **Khon** performances—traditional Thai masked dance performances depicting ancient stories—are available at venues like the **National Theatre** or **The Sala Chalermkrung Royal Theatre**.

  - **Vibe**: Cultural, elegant, and deeply rooted in Thai tradition.
  - **What to Expect**: Masked dances, music, and storytelling.

3.2. Cabaret Shows

Thailand's cabaret shows are famous worldwide for their vibrant performances, flamboyant costumes, and lively atmosphere. Whether in **Pattaya** or **Bangkok**, these shows are a fun and memorable experience.

- **Alcazar Cabaret (Pattaya)**: The **Alcazar Cabaret** in Pattaya is one of the most famous cabaret shows in Thailand. It features stunning performances with beautiful costumes, lip-sync performances, and a variety of music genres, from pop hits to traditional Thai songs.

- **Vibe**: Fun, flamboyant, and colorful.
- **What to Expect**: Lip-sync performances, dazzling costumes, and a lively atmosphere.

- **Calypso Cabaret (Bangkok)**: Located at the **Asiatique Riverfront**, **Calypso Cabaret** offers a glamorous and lively performance with a focus on drag shows and dazzling costumes. It's a must-see for those looking for an entertaining night out in Bangkok.

  - **Vibe**: Flashy, high-energy, and entertaining.
  - **What to Expect**: Colorful performances, catchy music, and a festive atmosphere.

Thailand's nightlife offers a diverse range of experiences to suit all types of travelers, whether you're in the mood for a quiet drink with a view, a lively night of dancing, or a cultural performance that showcases the country's rich heritage. From rooftop bars and beachside lounges to nightclubs and traditional shows, the options are endless. Whatever you choose, the nightlife in Thailand is sure to add excitement and memories to your journey.

7.3 Thai Massage and Spas: Relaxation at Its Best

Thailand is renowned worldwide for its massage and spa culture, which offers an unmatched combination of therapeutic benefits and relaxation. Traditional **Thai massage** is an ancient practice that blends acupressure, stretching, and yoga techniques to promote physical and mental well-being. Spas in Thailand often combine massage with other treatments, creating a luxurious and rejuvenating experience for visitors looking to unwind and restore balance to their body and mind.

In this section, we'll explore the different types of Thai massage, the best places to experience them, and the spa culture in Thailand, highlighting the importance of wellness and relaxation in Thai society.

1. Traditional Thai Massage

Traditional **Thai massage** (or **Nuad Thai**) is more than just a spa treatment—it is an ancient healing art that has been practiced for centuries. It is deeply rooted in Buddhist traditions and based on the concept of **energy lines** (or **Sen lines**), believed to flow throughout the body. The massage focuses on these energy lines, applying gentle pressure to specific points to unblock energy flow, relieve muscle tension, and promote overall health.

1.1. What to Expect from Thai Massage

Thai massage is typically performed on a mat on the floor, with the recipient fully clothed in loose, comfortable clothing. Unlike oil massages, Thai massage doesn't involve any oils or lotions. Instead, the therapist uses their hands, thumbs, elbows, knees, and feet to apply pressure along the body's energy lines.

- **Pressure**: Thai massage uses firm but gentle pressure, and you may be gently stretched or twisted into yoga-like postures. The technique involves rhythmic movements, gentle stretching, and pressure applied to key points along the body.

- **Duration**: A traditional Thai massage typically lasts between 60 and 90 minutes. During this time, you may feel a combination of relaxation and mild discomfort, particularly if your muscles are tight, but it should not be painful.

- **Benefits**: Thai massage can improve flexibility, relieve muscle tension, reduce stress, enhance circulation, and promote relaxation. It is especially beneficial for people with stiff muscles or those who engage in physical activities.

1.2. The Process of Thai Massage

- **Step 1**: A Thai massage typically starts with the client lying face up, and the therapist will begin

by gently stretching and massaging the legs, arms, and back.
- **Step 2**: The therapist may then use their palms, thumbs, and elbows to apply deeper pressure along the body's energy lines, focusing on key areas where tension accumulates (neck, shoulders, back).
- **Step 3**: The therapist will stretch and manipulate the body into various yoga-like poses to release tension and improve flexibility.
- **Step 4**: The session ends with the client lying face down or sitting as the therapist works on any remaining areas that require attention.

1.3. Best Places for Traditional Thai Massage

- **Wat Pho (Bangkok)**: The birthplace of Thai massage, **Wat Pho** (also known as the Temple of the Reclining Buddha) offers some of the most authentic and traditional massage experiences in the country. Located in the heart of Bangkok, the temple is home to the **Thai Traditional Medical and Massage School**, where visitors can receive a professional Thai massage from trained therapists. It's an excellent place to experience the art of Thai massage in its truest form.

- **Chiang Mai**: The northern city of **Chiang Mai** is also renowned for its Thai massage experiences, with numerous **traditional massage schools** and wellness centers offering services. The **Chiang Mai Traditional Massage School** is one of the most reputable places to learn or experience authentic Thai massage.

- **Koh Samui**: If you're relaxing on the beautiful beaches of **Koh Samui**, you can enjoy traditional Thai massage at **local spas** or **resort-based wellness centers**. Many beachfront resorts offer Thai massage services, making it easy to unwind with a view of the sea.

2. Spa Treatments in Thailand: Luxury and Wellness

Thailand is home to some of the world's most luxurious spas, offering a wide range of treatments that combine ancient traditions with modern wellness practices. From high-end spa resorts in places like **Phuket** and **Koh Samui** to local wellness centers, Thailand offers a variety of treatments designed to help you rejuvenate, relax, and recharge.

2.1. Popular Spa Treatments

- **Aromatherapy Massage**: This type of massage uses essential oils derived from plants to improve emotional and physical well-being. The oils are chosen based on your individual needs—whether you need to relax, rejuvenate, or relieve tension.

- **Herbal Compress Massage**: This is a traditional Thai treatment that uses a mixture of herbs and spices wrapped in a cloth compress. The compress is heated and applied to the body to relieve muscle tension, improve circulation, and promote relaxation.

- **Thai Foot Reflexology**: Focusing on pressure points on the feet that correspond to different areas of the body, **foot reflexology** is a popular Thai spa treatment aimed at relieving stress, improving circulation, and balancing energy.

- **Facial Treatments**: Many spas in Thailand offer facials using natural ingredients such as **papaya**, **coconut**, and **herbal infusions** to rejuvenate and cleanse the skin. These facials are often paired with massages to promote overall relaxation and wellness.

- **Body Scrubs**: Thailand's spas often offer invigorating body scrubs using natural ingredients like **sea salt**, **coffee**, or **herbal exfoliants**. These scrubs help remove dead skin cells, leaving your skin feeling soft and smooth.

2.2. Luxury Spas in Thailand

- **Anantara Spa (Koh Samui)**: Located within the luxury **Anantara Resort**, the **Anantara Spa** is known for offering traditional Thai massage alongside a full menu of luxurious treatments. Whether you're seeking a relaxing massage or an indulgent body wrap, this spa promises a tranquil environment with expert therapists.

- **Banyan Tree Spa (Phuket)**: The **Banyan Tree Spa** in **Phuket** offers a combination of Thai traditional therapies and modern treatments, set against the beautiful backdrop of lush greenery. Their **signature treatments** include relaxing massages, detoxifying body wraps, and facials that will leave you feeling pampered and refreshed.

- **Mandara Spa (Bangkok)**: Located in **Bangkok's Hilton Sukhumvit**, **Mandara Spa** combines luxurious treatments with Thai influences. Popular treatments include their aromatherapy massages and herbal compress therapies. The spa's serene atmosphere makes it a great place to relax after a day of sightseeing.

- **The Oasis Spa (Chiang Mai)**: **The Oasis Spa** offers a range of treatments that combine traditional Thai healing techniques with modern wellness practices. Set in a tranquil garden, the spa is renowned for its excellent service and relaxing ambiance. They offer everything from Thai massages to aromatherapy facials, making it a perfect escape for those looking for total relaxation.

2.3. Thai Spa Experience at Hotels and Resorts

Many high-end hotels and resorts in Thailand offer an in-house spa experience for their guests, providing convenience and luxury all in one place. These spa resorts provide a range of treatments, including traditional Thai massage, aromatherapy, body wraps, and beauty treatments. Here are some examples of spa-focused resorts:

- **Chiva-Som (Hua Hin)**: Known for its focus on health and wellness, **Chiva-Som** is a luxurious resort in **Hua Hin** that combines spa treatments with fitness, nutrition, and holistic therapies. Guests can enjoy a variety of wellness treatments, including detox programs, weight loss therapies, and stress-reduction techniques.

- **Kamalaya (Koh Samui)**: Located on **Koh Samui**, **Kamalaya** is a wellness sanctuary and holistic spa resort that blends traditional Eastern healing practices with Western treatments. The resort offers treatments for stress relief, detoxification, weight management, and rejuvenation, along with Thai massage and

Ayurvedic therapies.

3. Unique Wellness Experiences in Thailand

In addition to traditional spa treatments, Thailand offers unique wellness experiences that go beyond the typical massage. Many resorts and wellness centers offer customized programs designed to promote physical, emotional, and spiritual well-being.

3.1. Meditation and Mindfulness

Thailand is home to numerous **meditation centers** and **retreats** where visitors can practice mindfulness, meditation, and yoga. These retreats often take place in serene, natural settings, such as mountains, forests, or beachfront locations, providing a peaceful environment for mental relaxation and spiritual growth.

- **Wat Suan Mokkh (Chaiya)**: One of the most famous meditation centers in Thailand, **Wat Suan Mokkh** offers meditation retreats where participants can learn the basics of **Vipassana meditation** and spend days in silence, focusing on mindfulness and introspection.

- **The Yoga Studio (Koh Samui)**: For those looking to combine Thai massage with yoga, **The Yoga Studio** offers daily classes, workshops, and retreats. It's an ideal place to explore both physical fitness and mental clarity.

3.2. Detox and Wellness Retreats

Many spas and resorts in Thailand offer **detoxification programs** and **wellness retreats** that combine fasting, cleansing diets, and holistic treatments to rejuvenate your body and mind. These retreats are popular among travelers looking for a holistic approach to health and wellness.

- **The Sanctuary (Koh Phangan)**: Located on the island of **Koh Phangan, The Sanctuary** is a wellness center that offers detox programs, yoga, Thai massage, and cleansing diets. It's an excellent choice for those looking to cleanse their body and rejuvenate their spirit in a peaceful, natural environment.

- **Kamalaya Wellness Sanctuary (Koh Samui)**: This wellness resort offers personalized detox programs, with therapies designed to cleanse the body, reduce stress, and improve overall health. The treatments combine Thai massage with yoga, meditation, and detoxification to promote physical and emotional well-being.

Thailand's massage and spa culture offers a wealth of options for relaxation, rejuvenation, and wellness. Whether you're indulging in a traditional Thai massage, pampering yourself with a luxury spa treatment, or experiencing unique wellness retreats, Thailand provides everything you need to restore balance and unwind in one of the most tranquil settings in the world. Make time to experience the country's renowned wellness offerings for the ultimate relaxing escape.

7.4 Entertainment for Families: Theme Parks and Cultural Shows

Thailand is a family-friendly destination with a wide variety of entertainment options that cater to all ages. Whether you're seeking fun-filled adventures at world-class theme parks or looking to enjoy traditional cultural shows, Thailand has something to offer every family. These experiences are not only entertaining but also provide opportunities to learn about the country's rich culture, history, and natural beauty. In this section, we'll explore the best theme parks, cultural shows, and family-friendly activities that will make your trip to Thailand unforgettable.

1. Theme Parks: Fun for All Ages

Thailand boasts an array of theme parks that offer exciting adventures, thrilling rides, and interactive experiences. From large-scale amusement parks to water parks and animal-themed parks, there's no shortage of fun for families traveling with kids of all ages.

1.1. Dream World (Bangkok)

Located just outside of Bangkok, **Dream World** is a large theme park that offers a wide variety of rides, attractions, and live shows. The park is divided into different zones, including **Fantasy Land**, **Adventure Land**, and **Dream Garden**, making it suitable for all age groups.

- **Attractions**: Dream World features family-friendly attractions such as **Giant House**, where you can explore a world of optical illusions, and the **Snow Town**, a winter wonderland with real snow. There are also thrilling rides like the **Super Splash**, **Sky Coaster**, and **Space Mountain** for those seeking an adrenaline rush.

- **For Younger Kids**: The park also has gentler rides like **The Ferris Wheel**, **Bumper Cars**, and the **Cinderella Castle** for younger children.

- **Tips for Visiting**: Dream World is best visited during weekdays to avoid the crowds. It's also advisable to wear comfortable shoes, as the park is large and requires a lot of walking.

1.2. Siam Park City (Bangkok)

Known as the **largest water park** in Thailand, **Siam Park City** is a massive amusement and water park located in the heart of Bangkok. It features a combination of exciting water slides, theme park rides, and animal attractions, making it an ideal destination for a fun family day out.

- **Attractions**: The park is home to the **World's Largest Wave Pool**, a variety of water slides like **The Boomerang** and **The Speed Slide**, and a range of amusement rides, including roller coasters and bumper boats. The **Siam Carrousel** and **Family Roller Coaster** are also popular with younger visitors.

- **For Younger Kids**: The park has a designated **kiddie area** with gentle rides like **The Miniature Ferris Wheel** and **Dinosaur Land**, where kids can interact with life-sized dinosaur models.

- **Tips for Visiting**: Siam Park City can get crowded during holidays and weekends, so it's best to arrive early to avoid the lines. Don't forget to bring sunscreen and extra clothing if you plan to spend time in the water.

1.3. Cartoon Network Amazone Waterpark (Pattaya)

Located in **Pattaya**, the **Cartoon Network Amazone Waterpark** is an exciting water theme park that combines water slides with characters from the popular Cartoon Network shows. With more than 150 water attractions, this park is sure to delight kids and adults alike.

- **Attractions**: The park features **water rides**, **wave pools**, **lazy rivers**, and more. Popular attractions include **The Powerpuff Girls' Crazy River**, **The Adventure Time Water Slide**, and **The Lazy River**. For thrill-seekers, the **Omni Water Coaster** and **Mega Wave Pool** provide plenty of excitement.

- **For Younger Kids**: The park includes a **kid-friendly area** with smaller water slides, splash zones, and shallow pools, making it ideal for younger children to safely enjoy.

- **Tips for Visiting**: The park offers great deals on tickets for families, and it's often less crowded than other water parks in Thailand. Be sure to stay hydrated and take breaks in the shaded areas.

1.4. Safari World (Bangkok)

Safari World is one of Thailand's most popular family attractions. Located just outside of Bangkok, this wildlife park offers both a **Safari Park** and a **Marine Park**, allowing families to experience everything from animal encounters to thrilling performances.

- **Safari Park**: The **Safari Park** is home to over 100 species of animals, including lions, tigers, zebras, giraffes, and more. Visitors can drive through the park in their own vehicles or take a **safari bus tour** to observe the animals in a more natural, open setting.

- **Marine Park**: The **Marine Park** features a wide range of animal shows, including dolphin performances, sea lion shows, and an exciting **bird show**. There are also opportunities to feed animals like giraffes and elephants, making it an interactive experience for children.

- **Tips for Visiting**: Plan to spend the entire day at Safari World, as it offers a lot to see and do. Bring sunscreen, wear comfortable shoes, and prepare for a fun but full day of activities.

1.5. Khao Kheow Open Zoo (Chonburi)

Located just outside of Bangkok, the **Khao Kheow Open Zoo** is one of Thailand's largest zoos, focusing on conservation and wildlife education. The zoo is home to a wide variety of animals, including tigers, giraffes, zebras, and many endangered species.

- **Attractions**: The zoo offers unique experiences like **safari tours, animal shows**, and opportunities to interact with some animals. Kids can enjoy feeding giraffes, visiting the **Monkey Kingdom**, and exploring the zoo's beautiful botanical gardens.

- **For Younger Kids**: The zoo offers a **petting farm** where kids can interact with animals like goats, rabbits, and sheep, as well as a **playground** for them to burn off some energy.

- **Tips for Visiting**: The zoo is best visited in the cooler hours of the morning, as it can get hot in the afternoon. Don't forget to bring insect repellent and a camera to capture the wildlife experiences.

2. Cultural Shows and Performances: A Window into Thai Traditions

In addition to the fun and thrills of theme parks, Thailand offers a wealth of cultural performances that showcase the country's traditional dance, music, and theater. These shows are ideal for families looking to experience Thai culture in an entertaining and educational way.

2.1. Siam Niramit (Bangkok)

One of the most famous cultural performances in Thailand, **Siam Niramit** in **Bangkok** is a large-scale stage show that highlights Thailand's rich history, culture, and traditions. The show features **elaborate costumes**, **traditional Thai music**, and stunning **special effects**.

- **For Families**: The show is family-friendly, offering a captivating experience with amazing visuals and cultural storytelling. It takes visitors through Thailand's history, myths, and religious traditions.

- **What to Expect**: The show covers the three key aspects of Thai culture: **the Kingdom of Siam**, **the land of the gods**, and **the journey to the afterlife**. The performance is both educational and visually stunning, making it a great way for families to learn about Thai culture in an engaging way.

2.2. Cultural Shows in Chiang Mai: Khantoke Dinner and Traditional Dance

In **Chiang Mai**, families can enjoy traditional **Khantoke dinners** combined with cultural performances that showcase the dance, music, and traditions of the **Northern Thai** people.

- **Khantoke Dinner**: A Khantoke dinner is a traditional Northern Thai meal served on a circular tray with a variety of dishes such as sticky rice, curry, and vegetables. It's an immersive dining experience, often paired with live cultural performances.

- **Traditional Dance and Music**: While enjoying the meal, guests are entertained by **Lanna traditional dance**, **folk music**, and dramatic performances that highlight the region's cultural heritage.

2.3. Phuket FantaSea (Phuket)

Phuket FantaSea is a grand cultural show that combines Thai traditions with high-tech special effects, creating a dazzling performance. Set in a large theme park, the show tells the story of Thailand's rich culture through music, dance, and acrobatics.

- **What to Expect**: The show features a mix of traditional Thai dance, circus acts, and **elephant performances**. It's an engaging and exciting experience for children and adults alike, filled with color, music, and spectacular performances.

- **For Families**: Phuket FantaSea is designed to be fun for the whole family, with performances suitable for children, a variety of food stalls, and a lively atmosphere.

2.4. Thai Puppet Shows: Traditional Thai Puppetry (Bangkok and Chiang Mai)

For families with young children, **traditional Thai puppet shows** are a charming way to experience Thai culture. These shows often depict classic Thai stories and are performed using intricately crafted puppets.

- **What to Expect**: The puppet performances are often accompanied by live music and narration, providing an enchanting and unique glimpse into Thai art and storytelling.

- **Where to Watch**: Puppet shows can be found in cultural venues in **Bangkok**, such as **Joe Louis Puppet Theatre**, and in **Chiang Mai**, where some restaurants and cultural centers host puppet performances.

Thailand offers an incredible range of entertainment for families, from thrilling theme parks and waterparks to cultural performances that provide a deep dive into Thai traditions. Whether you're looking for exciting adventures or learning opportunities, these activities ensure that families of all sizes and ages will have a memorable and enjoyable time.

Made in the USA
Las Vegas, NV
17 April 2025